BLUE PULLMAN

BLUE PULLMAN

Kevin Robertson

Kestrel Railway Books

KRB Publications
PO Box 269
SOUTHAMPTON
SO30 4XR

www.krbpublications.co.uk

Printed by Cromwell Press

ISBN 0954485963

Front cover: An early trial run of a Western Region eight-coach set passing through Sonning Cutting on the approach to Reading in the period April to June 1960. This particular view was also used by the WR on at least one item of publicity material. *(PJ Hughes/Colour Rail)*

Title page: Derby, 9th June 1960, and a trial run of the new train attracts the attention of a number of youthful spotters. *(VR Webster/Kidderminster Railway Museum)*

CONTENTS

The first of Sam Lambert's striking views of the new Blue Pullman taken at Gorsey Bank crossing on the Wirksworth Branch in the winter of 1959/60. (The lightly-used former Midland line between Bedford and Hitchin, which eventually closed in 1962, was similarly used for both low-speed trial running trials and photography.) Sam Lambert of 'Design' magazine, was responsible for a number of the publicity views of the period. Several similar photographs of the front of the trains have been located, some with the background masked out although, as here, the giveaway is often the reflection on the front. Almost the only things that spoil the neat look of the front are the brackets for the old-style oil lamps, whose addition and placing appears to be very much an afterthought. With just two oil-lamp brackets, not every headlamp code could be displayed, but as the sets were intended only to run as Class A this hardly mattered. Notice the wording under the left-hand buffer that reads "Shore supply 400 volts".

Western Region advertising. Although undated, this is believed to be post 1963. This was a simple folded card containing an illustration and the times of the relevant services. The covers are black on gold.

(Antony M Ford Collection)

PREFACE, ACKNOWLEDGMENTS and BIBLIOGRAPHY

In setting out the story of the Blue Pullman trains, I feel that once again I am almost putting my head into the proverbial lion's mouth. In my naivety when I started this work, I might have considered that the history of just five sets over just a thirteen-year period would warrant, perhaps, little more than a few thousand words. How wrong I was!

Having read various published sources, it was soon clear that there were gaps in the information recounted - gaps that could not be ignored. At the same time, various writers over the years had reported totally different conclusions – although, may I say immediately, I am sure that most were recounted with the best of intentions.

There was therefore but one option, to go back to primary sources, and start again from the outset. But here I had a significant advantage over my predecessors, as much of what had been written in the past was published before 2003, and it was in 2003 that several files relating to the trains were released into the public domain from the National Archive. This was the start that was needed, and it has led along a number of different routes to culminate in what I hope is as full a picture as it is presently possible to make on the history, operation, and demise of these unique trains.

As intimated above, the final result is very different from what I had originally envisaged, and this is due in no small part to the assistance given by The Pullman Society, and in particular Charles Long and Anthony Ford. In the case of the former, I knew I had arrived at the correct location for our meeting by the presence of a Pullman armchair in the hallway - the rest of the house being similarly adorned with Pullman paraphernalia. Antony Ford, as Curator and Archivist of The Pullman Society, willingly allowed both access to and the loan of much irreplaceable paperwork and advertising material relative to this story. Much is reproduced within these pages. To attempt to record anything on Pullmans within the UK without the assistance of these gentleman and The Pullman Society would be nothing short of foolhardy. I can therefore do no more than earnestly recommend anyone with more than a passing interest in Pullman vehicles and services to seriously consider joining this august group. (The Membership Secretary can be contacted at 140 St Helens Down, HASTINGS, TN34 2AR, or alternatively at: awood17166@aol.com.) All unaccredited photographs are from the author's collection and were taken by persons unknown.

Having also been involved in railway research for, shall we say, 'a few years', I am fortunate to have built up a number of friends, that one only has pick up the phone and call for assistance to be provided. In the same way a number of new friends have been made, and to each of these, I can only offer my sincere thanks and gratitude. I may have compiled the book, but it is you who have made it possible.

In alphabetical order, many thanks indeed to: Neville Bridger for finding some excellent archive paperwork, Peter Brumby, David Canning, Neal Couzens, Adrian Curtis (whose own work on recording the history of BR diesel classes has set new standards), Peter Dobson, Michael Farr, David Hyde (not just a Great Western expert), Kidderminster Railway Museum in particular Audie Baker and David Postle, Stuart MacKay, Mike Mensing (thank you for placing your collection at my disposal), Julian Peters (for access to the collection of the late Ivo Peters), Neal Ruffles, Ian Shawyer (what does one say when the comment is, "Oh, I've got a poster for them at home. Would you like to borrow it?"), Adrian Vaughan (is there anything this man has not got a photo of?), Pete Waterman (a sincere vote of thanks), Chris Webb, Nick Wheat, and of course, the redoubtable Ron White at Colour Rail – what would we do without him? There is also an excellent Blue Pullman discussion group on the Internet (blue_pullman-owner@yahoogroups.com). No doubt there is someone I have forgotten, my sincere apologies and gratitude to you, nevertheless.

Special thanks are also due to my partners at Kestrel Railway Books, Howard and Clare Sprenger. It is thanks to their encouragement, cajoling, constructive criticism, and above all endless cups of tea and e-mails that have made all of this possible, as well as finding additional sources of information from their own network of contacts.

Of the published sources consulted, these are numerous and varied. Some contain little more than a few lines, and others have much detail. Where it is relevant, some source references are referred to within the text. The following books and magazines, however, have been consulted in a more general sense:

Backtrack, various issues.
British Rail 1948 – 1978 A Journey by Design, Brian Haresnape, Ian Allan, 1979
British Rail DMUs & Diesel Railcars, Brian Morrison, Ian Allan, 1998
British Rail Mark 2 Coaches, Michael Harris, Mallard/Venture
Bristol Railway Panorama, Colin Maggs, Millstream Books, 1990
British Railways Illustrated, various issues of magazines and annuals, Irwell Press
British Railways Midland Region Magazine, various issues
British Railways Mark 1 Coaches, David Parkin, Historical Model Railway Society
British Railways Western Region Magazine, various issues
Locospotters Annual 1962, G Freeman Allen, Ian Allan, 1962
Metro-Cammell, 150 years of Craftsmanship, Keith Beddoes et al, Runpast, 1999
Modern Railways, various issues
Modern Railways Profile No 10, Ian Allan (Pub), 1985
On and Off the Rails, John Elliot, George Allen and Unwin, 1982
A Pictorial Record of British Railways Diesel Multiple Units, Brian Golding, Cheona Publications, 1995

Pullman in Europe, George Behrend, Ian Allan, 1962
Pullman Trains in Britain, RW Kidner, Oakwood Press, 1998
The Railway Magazine, various issues
The Railway Observer, various issues
Railways on the Screen, John Huntley, Ian Allan, 1993
Traction Magazine, various issues
The Western Since 1948, G Freeman Allen, Ian Allan, 1979

Several commercially available video tapes have been produced in recent years, showing the Blue Pullmans in service – sometimes the same piece of film appearing on more than one tape. These are recommended to those readers who may wish to view a Blue Pullman in action.

Sadly, the one archive not to have been fully explored is that of the builder, Metropolitan-Cammel. Over the years though, copies of much of this material appears to have been made and has passed to private collectors, indeed it was just such an item, that really started the author on the trail of the trains. The official archive has fortunately survived, and has passed to the care and stewardship of the Historical Model Railway Society. As yet, and for the foreseeable future, it is not open for inspection, and it might therefore still reveal more in years to come. I would encourage future historians to study this material as and when it is eventually released.

The story of the Blue Pullmans is one where I have at times drawn comparisons with other forms of motive power, some of whose history I have also recorded in book form. Previous writers have often drawn comparisons with the more recent HST sets, and regard the Blue Pullmans as their true ancestors, but I cannot say that I totally agree. Yes there are some similarities, but there are also similarities between the story of the Blue Pullmans and the reasons why Bulleid's "Leader" failed so dramatically just a few years earlier. (Read the text to find out how and why!) If the connection between Blue Pullman and "Leader" is proven (as I believe it is), imagine now a connection between Blue Pullman and the HST, leading to an even more remote connection between "Leader" and the HST! No - the connection between differing forms of traction is, and always has been, tenuous. Each must be regarded as having its own place in history, and should therefore be viewed as an individual item.

In the pages that follow, I sincerely hope I have been able to do justice to a remarkable train. I have attempted to form a connection between fact and folklore, and in so doing have produced a cohesive link between the text and the prototype. What follows is a ride, at times rough (just like the prototype), and at other times smooth.

Kevin Robertson,
Southampton 2005

M60093 at an unidentified location.   *(Rod Blencowe Collection)*

INTRODUCTION

Born as a consequence of the 1955 British Railways Modernisation Plan, it is now more than three decades since the Blue Pullman units operated on British Railways. Three decades (the actual year was 1973) when the last train ran to and from Paddington, and fast approaching four decades since the sets operated on the Midland Main Line out of St Pancras.

To some, the Blue Pullman sets have been almost idolised and seen as forerunners to the HST High Speed Trains. The five Blue Pullman trains were conceived and built as undoubted flagships, as far as luxury travel by train in the UK was concerned. For years too, they have also been referred to as the first multiple unit Pullman trains in the world – not so, remember the electric Brighton Belle sets? It would be more accurate to describe them as the first diesel multiple-unit Pullman sets in the world, and perhaps more poignantly, the last multiple-unit Pullman sets (up to now at least). Certainly at the time of their introduction there was much media hype and pomp surrounding the new trains, together with, it must be said, a genuine attempt to ensure that the sets were a commercial success.

To those reading this, who are perhaps expecting the narrative to roundly condemn the trains, there will be disappointment, for in many respects, the Blue Pullman sets were both a mechanical and a commercial success. However, in both of these areas there were also major problems, problems that British Railways Management conveniently chose to ignore, rather than address, at the time. These areas are all discussed in detail in the chapters that follow.

Up until now, writers who have committed themselves to recording the history of the trains have mainly concentrated in particular areas, the controversy surrounding the rough riding being one classic example. But there is so much more to say on the subject as a whole, particularly as some papers pertaining to their history were marked "Closed until 2003", and were only released for public inspection at the National Archive (previously the Public Record Office) from that date.

What I have set out to record is as complete a history as I have been able to determine. This has involved recourse to a number of primary, as well as secondary sources, and also to personal interviews (actual references are mentioned in the Preface, Acknowledgements and Bibliography). As with my previous books on what might be deemed "touchy" issues (notably Bulleid's Leader, and the GWR Gas Turbines) I seek neither to praise nor condemn the Blue Pullmans, but to make as many facts available as possible, and leave it to the reader to decide upon their own viewpoint. More than one conclusion is possible, it is for the reader to choose which they wish to subscribe to.

The unravelling of what I hope then is the full story of the Blue Pullman trains has been a project that has given me great pleasure. I only hope the final result will give the reader equal pleasure.

The Western Region of British Railways **and** *The Pullman Car Company*

request the pleasure of the company of

*on Monday 5th September 1960
on the occasion of a special run of the
new Pullman Diesel Express train
for the journey
from London (Paddington) to Swindon and back*

Luncheon en route
Kindly bring this
card with you

R.S.V.P. (by August 17th, 1960)
to General Manager, Western Region,
Paddington Station, London, W.2

FOR TRAIN TIMINGS PLEASE SEE REVERSE SIDE

An original invitation card, printed in black on a cream background with the BR and Pullman emblems in light green, with the whole edged in gold. At least one other similar card was issued for a run the very next day from Bristol to Reading and back.

(Antony M Ford Collection)

Chapter 1

A BOLD AMBITION

Britain needed some good news in early July 1960. So far, the headlines had been dominated by an all-Australian men's final at Wimbledon on 2nd July, whilst the very next day another Australian, Jack Brabham had romped to victory in the French Grand Prix. Now was the time for Britain to shine (quite literally) as on Monday 4th July 1960 a gleaming new train, The Midland Pullman, commenced running between Manchester and London (St Pancras) as the unchallenged flagship of luxury travel on the railway network.

Much was riding on the success of the venture - finance, prestige, arguably even future financial investment, for the new train was a genuine attempt to not only win back lost passenger revenue, but also to attract new patronage.

1960 was also five years on from the announcement of the modernisation of Britain's railways, which as far as many enthusiasts are concerned, is restricted to a commitment to the abolition of steam traction, and its replacement with more modern motive power. But the building of new locomotives was only one small part of the whole modernisation concept, and while the Blue Pullman trains might well have much of their origins in that 1955 Modernisation Plan, their actual ancestry and the concept that led up to their approval for development can be traced back to the previous year, and more accurately, 11th October 1954.

On this date, Hugh Barker, a part-time member of the British Transport Commission, compiled a memorandum in which he suggested that the BTC's acquisition of a controlling interest in the Pullman Car Company, allied to the development of DMU (diesel multiple unit) operation, provided an opportunity for the provision of prestige inter-city services, "to catch the imagination of the public, and give a visible demonstration of the new potentialities of rail travel."

Three months later, in January 1955, came the £1.2bn Modernisation Plan which led, on 14th June 1955, to the establishment of a committee to report on the proposed introduction of DMU main line express trains, "within, say, the next five years for operation on services such as the following: London-Leeds, London-Manchester, London-Birmingham and London-Bristol". At this stage the reference to Pullman is not made, that would come later, but it is also interesting to note that the subsequent Blue Pullman trains would indeed operate on three of the four routes suggested at that time.

The establishment of the formal committee was really the suggestion of Hugh Barker of the BTC, and according to Charles Long of The Pullman Society, Barker had in mind an extension of the type of multiple-unit express Pullman service such as the Brighton Belle. Motive power was not specified, but Barker's note to the BTC of

October 1954 had commented on a possible Birmingham Belle, Manchester Belle and Leeds Belle. (It has been previously suggested by a number of authors that the Blue Pullman trains were modelled on the original Trans-Europe Express trains. This is not based on fact, however, but each had its origins around the same time, and both were similar as far as multiple-unit operation was concerned. The TEE entered service in 1957, but the original units did not offer the same "at seat" meal service that was later provided in the British trains.) Barker was certainly ahead of his time in his thinking, and while he has never been formally credited as such, it may be said that he was the true progenitor of the Blue Pullman trains. (Barker's subsequent involvement in discussions is not reported, and neither has any detail been discovered about the time he time spent with the BTC.)

Ten members comprised what was officially known as the Diesel Multiple Unit Main Line Express Committee, the participants having been proposed by AJ Pearson, Chief of General Duties on the BTC, whose own career had started on the Cheshire Lines Committee. It appears that Pearson was astute enough to arrange for a cross-section of individuals, who would bring varying experience with them, as well as being of broadly (a word chosen deliberately here, as will become apparent later) similar character. Chaired by Herbert Phillips, Assistant General Manager of the Western Region, the group was sometimes referred to as the Phillips Committee. Other members included WP Allen, David Blee, Michael Bonavia, Roland C Bond, JR Pike, and SB Warder; Peter A Keen acted as secretary, and in addition, EK Portman-Davis was involved as catering consultant, when necessary.

Presumably, it was Pearson, on behalf of the BTC, who set out the terms of reference within which the committee would work:

"Economic operation would require an extremely rapid turn-round, and new and accelerated methods of servicing, fuelling and maintenance at terminals. (The committee inferred that to achieve this requirement, stock and locomotive shunting movements should be abolished. It was then a small step to recognising that multiple-unit operation was the ideal.)

"The trains will succeed only if they offer great strides forward in speed, comfort and convenience, and punctuality must be taken for granted.

"There should be a maximum speed of 100mph, and a start–to–stop average not less than 60mph.

"Comfort, with which is associated personal service to passengers, must vie with airline standards. Appearance and décor must be ultra-modern. They should run at times suitable to businessmen. The public will be pre-

Facing page: The final result of the 1955 discussions for a luxury train service - an 8-car set operates the 4.50pm Paddington to Wolverhampton service near West Wycombe. The driver's sun-visor can easily be seen. *(HK Harman)*

pared to pay a surcharge for this service, but this should not exceed Pullman charges."

Looking back over fifty years, these were bold statements indeed. Several aspects of the remit are taken for granted nowadays, but were totally radical ideas for the period – maintenance at terminals being just one aspect, that in turn, would lead to the provision of "shore supplies".

The suggestion of expected speeds is also worth discussing. It should be stated straight away that the figures quoted were a hoped-for projection for the future (no actual date was suggested when such running would be possible). The practicalities of running at such speeds would have been very clear to the Committee, the most obvious being the difficult matter of ensuring a clear path. Limitations with contemporary mechanical signalling had resulted in double-block working for the pre-war LNER streamlined expresses, and the timekeeping of the LMR flagship trains was at best described as "poor". The only other region involved, the Western, had ensured that its fastest trains were run outside peak times when there was little chance of delay caused by other services being "out of course". To encourage business travel would mean running at high speeds at peak times. It was a bold ambition.

The reference to Pullman is also interesting, as this is the first time the name occurs, although it would be some time before the criteria were met that would allow the new trains to appear under the Pullman banner. Also interesting is the question of a surcharge for what eventually became a slower service, resulting in complaints from disgruntled passengers on the Western Region.

Now it is time to explain to the reference to the word "broad" made earlier. As mentioned, the Committee Chairman was Herbert Phillips, who had spent almost the whole of his railway career with the Great Western Railway. Separate from the recommendations of the Committee as a whole, Phillips also submitted his view that any new train intended to run on the WR should be built to the full extent of the loading gauge allowed on that region, which at 9ft 7in wide (based on the former broad gauge) was 7in wider than permitted elsewhere. This, he argued, would allow for "2+2" seating in second class, and therefore accommodate additional passengers. Committee member David Blee, who became Chairman of the LMR at the time the trains were introduced, and who is referred to again in Chapter 5, was another former GWR man, but it appears that he did not back Phillips' proposal. As might be expected, the suggestion was rejected by the BTC, as the projected new trains were seen as experimental, and could not be guaranteed to be restricted to the same routes for the whole of their working lives. It was a logical and perfectly understandable response from the BTC, and one that was also prophetic for the future.

Phillips also made a second suggestion, which made more sense, relating to the future WR sets having hydraulic transmission. Here the reader might be excused

for thinking that this WR man still had his mind set in GWR days, and simply wanted to be different from everyone else. This was not the case, as I recounted in my 1989 book *The Great Western Railway Gas Turbines – a Myth Exposed*:

"...that is not to say the gas turbines did not pass on anything to the new generation of motive power, for the use of hydraulic transmission was a direct development of Nos 18000 and 18100, the desire being to dispense with the apparent unreliability of the electric transmission both engines possessed. In essence this was a viable and carefully considered viewpoint, for had not both engines suffered a number of electrically-derived faults ranging from generator flashovers to traction motor failures and bogie fires? In defence of the electrical engineers though, it must be said that the last-named problems were aggravated by ignorance, the railways seemingly unaware of the essential criteria in keeping the bogies and associated traction motors free from a built up of oil and dirt, a difficult task indeed when servicing facilities were dependent upon the conditions existing in a steam shed."

An additional benefit in favour of hydraulic transmission related to weight saving. Early on in the Committee's discussions, there was some doubt over the power output that could be derived from the diesel engines available at the time, and this might have limited the ability of any new unit to maintain the desired schedules. The weight saving possible with hydraulic transmission was seen by the WR as a way of increasing the power-to-weight ratio. Even so, as early as 1956, before the first of the hydraulic main line diesels had been delivered to the WR, this form of technology was viewed unfavourably by the BTC. (Why and how the WR managed to continue in the pursuit and development of main line diesel hydraulic engines to replace steam is out of place in this narrative. Suffice to say a 2000hp Warship diesel for the WR with hydraulic transmission tipped the scales at just under 80 tons, whilst the nearest contemporary single-engined, diesel-electric equivalent was the Class 40, introduced in 1958, which had the same power output, but weighed in at a massive 133 tons.)

Phillips might have had the mindset of a former GWR man as far as wider vehicles were concerned, but not in relation to the difficulties associated with electrical transmission. In the event, any electrical problems with the new trains were no more than might have been expected with a new design, although it is interesting to note that, half a century later, there are newly-built trains (not Pullman of course) running around with diesel-hydraulic transmission.

To return to 1955, it would appear that once set up, there was much movement behind the scenes amongst the Committee, as it was able to present its first major report as early as 23rd August 1955. It reported that, "it would be necessary to formulate one or two pilot schemes to enable the practical advantages, particularly as to utilisation, to be assessed, and the London Midland and Western Regions are now exploring the possibility of running trains of the type envisaged. Services between London and

Manchester, Birmingham and Bristol are being considered." The same report also showed that the Committee had already settled on just two options for train formation, a six-coach set for first class only and an eight-coach set with accommodation equally divided between first and second class.

This first report indicated that the routes used would be over LMR and WR metals, so the management, or at least the traffic departments, of these regions became involved as a result. Prior to the second formal meeting of the Committee, held on 3rd November 1955, each region had submitted its view on the Committee's ideas - the Western claiming that better utilisation of stock could be achieved with a conventional locomotive-hauled train, while the Midland proclaimed a preference for a multitude of services that included Euston to Glasgow and St Pancras to Leicester, Nottingham and Derby. At the same time, one member of the Committee (it was is not stated who) requested that the LMR look into the possibility of an early morning Leeds to St Pancras train.

These representations to the Committee are worthy of some exploration as they indicate a distinctly independent stance by both regions concerned. The WR seems to have conveniently ignored one of the main criteria for the proposed new trains, and while no attempt will be made to explain this here, it is worth recording that just a few months earlier, in June 1955, a new steam-hauled Pullman service, the South Wales Pullman, had been inaugurated between Paddington and Swansea. The response of the LMR is altogether more surprising, and it also appears to have hardly considered any of the criteria that it was informed of, since the Glasgow service was impossible at the time if the desired speeds were to be achieved. (Did the London-Glasgow proposal have any bearing on the introduction of the 1957 lightweight steam-hauled Caledonian service?) Leeds was discounted as a destination due to operational difficulties that included severe speed restrictions in the area caused by mining subsidence, and at around the same time a separate proposal to base the new trains at Sheffield was ruled out for similar reasons.

It has been popular (and at times, truthful) to deride the Western Region for its independent stance following Nationalisation, so much so that it was often referred to as the "Great Western Region". The most obvious departure from the norm was the widespread use of a pseudo-GWR livery on its locomotives and rolling stock. However, in the case of the Blue Pullman, it is the London Midland that is more deserving of criticism. Contemporary LMR management (names are deliberately not mentioned) appeared to have totally ignored the full potential offered by their alternative lines to London, and Pullman aspirations were seemingly confined to the former LNWR line in and out of Euston, with scant regard being paid to the opportunity presented by the Midland line from St Pancras. Indeed the LMR, although recognising Manchester as a likely source of potential revenue for the new service, was of the opinion that the trains could not run from Manchester to Euston due "operational difficulties". When pushed, however, they insisted that

this was due to the lack of available paths, hence a scheme was put forward for a single unit to cover a four-leg circuit based on Derby comprising Derby to St Pancras, St Pancras to Nottingham, Nottingham to St Pancras and St Pancras to Derby.

No consideration was apparently given by the LMR to the use of the Midland line to and from Manchester - a fact that was commented on by Michael Bonavia in his book, *British Rail: The First 25 Years* as something that, "outraged common sense". (Bonavia was a serving member of the Phillips Committee.) The fact that the trains did eventually serve Manchester was due in no small part to the efforts of the Committee's secretary, Peter Keen (a future Chief Passenger Manager on BR) who, having carefully studied the working timetables, was able to demonstrate that it was perfectly feasible to find paths for the new service over the Midland line between Manchester and St Pancras at the required times. (Some element of Crewe versus Derby here? Derby was thought to have ruled the roost under the LMS, but after Nationalisation, power swung back towards Crewe – perhaps they were getting their own back a little!)

However, there was another more sinister reason why LMR management was reluctant to consider Manchester as a base for the new units at that time, and this was their fear that if Manchester were chosen, major industrial relations problems could lie ahead. Charles Long recalls the north-west having, "the presence of a hard knot of militant members of the NUR among Manchester-based restaurant-car staff." He is also of the opinion that the threat of strike action forced the indefinite postponement of the planned service launch from January 1960, but this was more likely due to other unrelated issues, as will be recounted later.

It would be tempting to suggest that this lack of thought over routing, or the fears of Union hostility by the LMR, were respectively an oversight and an over-reaction, but both views must be questioned. Some of the best brains on the railway were serving on, or accessible to, the Committee, and one inevitable conclusion to be reached is that factions within the LMR were turning away from the idea of a prestige service in favour of concentrating resources on the electrification of the LNWR route, which was to be in the first-wave of such upgrading, and was due to be completed around the same time as the East Coast Main Line scheme.

A most important result of the November meeting was a set of outline drawings giving various options for projected six- and eight-coach sets, having either under-floor or above-floor engines. It is in this area where the previously incorrect assumption that continental practice influenced the Blue Pullman trains might have originated; the only true comparison related to the choice of power units. Up until then, multiple-unit trains in Britain had been equipped with bus-type under-floor engines that provided sufficient power only for secondary and branch line use. The new service with 100mph (maximum) and 60mph (average) speeds would demand significantly more output, and such engines were not available locally

The fact that both 6- and 8-car sets were symmetrical as far as each half-set was concerned, was intended to allow for just part of a train to be withdrawn for maintenance from time to time. In practice this would only really have worked if a far greater number of sets had been built, so photographs of half-sets are rare. This is a view of a half-set, led by M60091, possibly at Derby on an unreported date. Moving ahead some years, it has been reported that on the WR in the late 1960s, an 8-car train was, for a time, formed of one half-set in original blue and white and another half-set in white and blue.

at that time, hence the search overseas for inspiration. (Surviving files at The National Archive include a brochure on the contemporary American "Aero-Train", but whether this was an attempted sales drive by the manufacturers, or whether it was simply the result of a trawl by the BTC through the latest railway technology is not clear; probably more the latter.)

Exactly where this search for suitable engines took the Committee is not recorded, but it eventually settled on German-designed MAN 1000hp engines, which would be built in the UK under licence by the North British Locomotive Company. Regardless of the number of coaches, the new trains would comprise two power cars, one at each end, giving each set a total power output of 2000hp.

It is likely that at this stage, RC Bond, as one of the engineering members of the Committee, was able to calculate the likely power-to-weight ratio of the new trains, and relate them to the speeds required. No paperwork has been found to substantiate this, but it is also likely that various strategic decisions were made at this

time, for example, that the trains would be equipped with auxiliary engines to supply power for catering and air-conditioning (although, exactly when this feature was decided upon is not recorded), and also the important question of scheduling. Regardless of available paths, the power output was considered insufficient for the hoped-for maximum of 100mph, so hereafter, 90mph was settled upon. Even so, there were still fears that 2000hp would be insufficient for an eight-coach set, and it was even suggested that all the sets be restricted to a maximum of six-cars. (Similar NBL/MAN engines were installed in the 1958 Warship class diesels, and also in D833-D865 of the 1960 Warship class.)

The same plans show passenger seating that both revolved and reclined, and included clip-on trays for meal service. Each train, regardless of whether it was formed with six or eight cars, was fitted with centre doors, and was symmetrical in the layout of its accommodation. (Each half was actually a "mirror" of the other, since the kitchen, toilets and double seats were all on the same side;

this is best seen in the accompanying plan.) In the six-car train, the first three cars were, motor first, kitchen first and open first, with the second set of three being (in reverse) open first, kitchen first and finally, motor first. The eight-car sets had a motor second followed by an open second, with the last two cars of each four-car half-set being identical to vehicles two and three in the six-car formation. At this stage the length of each vehicle was specified at 64ft 6in, but in practice, this would increase by some two feet. In other areas there were close similarities with the vehicles as actually built, although some variations in the seating accommodation were introduced.

On-train catering now moves centre-stage, although it should be said that this subject does becomes somewhat convoluted. Around this time, Phillips as Chairman of the Committee contacted Colonel Frank Harding, the General Manager of the Pullman Car Co, and EK Portman-Dixon, Chief of Restaurant Cars at the BTC. It appears that the BTC Committee was actively investigating a totally radical approach to catering on the new trains, involving the use of pre-packaged frozen foods that would have been reheated as with airline catering. (It is not known whether this would have involved pre-packed set meals, or whether a varied menu would still have been provided.) It appears that the aim of these discussions was to establish whether or not this form of catering might save space which could then be given over to additional seating.

Related to this same topic, although not explicitly mentioned anywhere, is the decision that, not only was some form of catering desirable, but that it should be an "at-your-seat" service, that implied far more than the conventional kitchen/restaurant car service available on most principle services. The exceptions were, of course, the established Pullman trains, and the known contact with Col Harding implies that the decision had already been made that the new trains should be Pullman-based. It is strange that this important issue is not more explicitly referred to within the various Committee minutes.

The saving of space in order to increase the amount of seating was a valid and relevant issue. Consider a train of, say, ten vehicles comprising eight first or composite vehicles plus a restaurant car and a kitchen car. The last-named might be the most weighty at perhaps 40 tons and the rest perhaps 30 to 35 tons apiece, giving a total net weight of perhaps 320 tons. Two of those vehicles (the kitchen and restaurant cars) perhaps amounting to 75 tons together, would be devoted solely to occasional use. Revenue from on-train catering would have to cover the wear and tear and depreciation of these vehicles, catering staff wages, and the wholesale cost of the food and drink, and a proportion would also have to go towards infrastructure financing. Little wonder that the railway looked for means of guaranteeing a greater return on vehicle and running costs than that provided by the vagaries of catering.

A later 1960s comment (which was probably equally applicable in the 1950s) stated that the proportion of passengers on Pullman services partaking of all kinds of refreshments was greater than on services where the travelling public had the choice of visiting the restaurant/buffet car, or being served at their seat.

Returning to the suggestion to serve frozen meals, a response from the Pullman Car Company has not come to light, but the General Manager of the BTC Hotels and Catering service, Frank Hole (to whom Portman-Dixon reported), was known to be enthusiastic. He did, however, express the opinion that Pullman might not want to be associated with what would be seen as a lessening in standards (again there is the inference that the decision had already been made to make the new trains Pullman-based). Nevertheless, Portman-Dixon was tasked with investigating the practical issues involved, and he subsequently reported that he could not guarantee any significant savings by using frozen food, the comparative figures being a cost of 77.5p per head for a meal based on conventional cooking and £1.00 for a frozen meal.

Although it is not mentioned, he no doubt based his results on the fact that a conventional oven would still be needed to reheat the frozen food, and would therefore occupy the same space. Today that may be a little difficult to understand, but the microwave oven, whose origins can be traced back to the development of RADAR in World War II, had only been commercially available since 1954, and even then at a size and price that was only suited to very large commercial catering institutions. It would be the early 1970s before an everyday domestic appliance became widely available and affordable. The recent reduction in the number of kitchen cars on the railway owes as much to a travel and social lifestyle changes, as it does to the space savings of the microwave cooker!

Away from the aroma of cooking, the next major report from the Committee to have been located was presented to the BTC on 25th July 1956 (later recorded as BTC Minute 9/384). This included a number of interesting proposals, one of which had originated from an LMR suggestion of 30th December 1955, that saw the new trains being based at Derby rather than Manchester, and proposed a four-trip daily itinerary: Derby to St Pancras, St Pancras to Nottingham, Nottingham to St Pancras and St Pancras to Derby. The same report also vetoed the suggested London to Leeds route, due to the fact that this was being given priority for electrification in the 1955 Modernisation Plan. We shall return to the proposal for the suggested Leeds service later.

To be fair, whichever locations and times were eventually chosen, there would inevitably be a compromise. A morning start from Manchester arriving in London mid- to late-morning, was not considered suitable for all, and it was recognised that there would be those who would find alternative means to reach the Capital in time for an early-morning meeting. However, by setting the departure time from St Pancras (as was later accomplished) at just after 6.00pm, most business meetings would be concluded by then, and the train would allow for a return trip with dinner taken in comfort.

The July 1956 report, consisting of more than 30 paragraphs, covered a variety of topics, including

thoughts on the number of cars that were considered desirable, the proportion of first to second class accommodation (third class had been officially designated as second class in May 1956) and the types and methods of propulsion. As would be expected, the subject of on-board catering was again discussed, and while this might perhaps appear to be an indigestion-inducing amount of narrative on a dietary subject, it is worth continuing as the emphasis at this time appeared to be moving away from any Pullman involvement.

The report noted that, "The General Manager of the Pullman Car Co (Col Harding), has been consulted, and has agreed that the catering accommodation proposed is adequate." It continued, "The possibility that the Pullman Car Co might provide the catering on these services has been considered, and while it would be possible for this to be done, the General Manager of the Pullman Car Co does not consider it desirable that his company should undertake the work, since it does not maintain establishments at any of the points on which the service will be based. It is therefore recommended that catering should be undertaken by the Restaurant Car Service. The Chief of Restaurant Cars and Refreshment Rooms is in agreement with this recommendation. Since it is not recommended that the Pullman Car Co should provide catering on these services, it would not be appropriate to apply the name "Pullman" to them. It is felt that the service will be sufficiently distinctive if the trains are not named".

Clearly there was still a long way to go before the Committee reached any decision that the trains would appear in the form in which they were later remembered, but here is one final comment pertaining to Col Harding that is best described in the words of Charles Long in his article *Fact, Fiction, and Pullman Folklore* which appeared in the *Pullman Society Journal*.

"As set out here, Col Harding's reasoning seems odd. Equally, of course, the (Pullman) company did 'not maintain establishments' in Newcastle, Bradford, Harrogate, Hull or Sheffield, but it had no problem in supplying the 'Tees-Tyne', 'Yorkshire' and (later) 'Master Cutler' Pullman trains on arrival at Kings Cross by a van service from its commissary depot in Battersea – as, indeed, was to happen also at St Pancras and Paddington when the 'Blue Pullmans' were eventually introduced in 1960. Could it be that Pullman's General Manager had simply misunderstood what he had originally been told about the routing of the new trains, and he thought that it was proposed to run them between Manchester, Birmingham and Bristol (or some other provincial centre)? It has been said that the good Colonel managed to get hold of the wrong end of the stick on at least two occasions that I can clearly recall. There was the time, when, returning from a visit to Kings Cross, he burst into the Traffic Superintendent's Office at Victoria, plainly much agitated, and announced that he had just seen 'Topaz' in the 'Queen of Scots' when it should be in the Transport Museum (then at Clapham). I'm still not quite sure whether he really believed an assurance that one of the 1960-built cars had taken the same name as the preserved 1914 vehicle. On another occasion, having been told that (bearing in mind the low seat capacity of 'classic' first-class Pullmans) the provision of a special train for upwards of 350 passengers would be quite impractical, he came in with a copy of LTC Rolt's book *Red for Danger*, and triumphantly pointed out that the West Coast express derailed at Wigan in August 1873 had 25 coaches in all. 'If the railways could run such long trains then they can surely do it now'. It had evidently not occurred to him that main-line trains were at that point in the 19th century formed exclusively of lightweight and often very flimsy four and six wheel coaches."

It might appear that the subject of catering was of paramount importance compared with the actual selection of routes, design of stock and mechanical matters, but the success of the proposed new service was dependent upon attracting the right clientele, and accordingly, the catering arrangements had to be just right.

According to the Committee, the notion of retaining the catering under the control of BTC Hotels and Catering, was agreed, and this became its recommendation. However, the conclusion of the Committee was only one of the ideas that the BTC had to consider, as it had also requested a feasibility report from its own Traffic Survey Group (TSG) in the form of what would today be termed "market research". Little appears in the minutes pertaining to the establishment or make-up of the TSG, so it could be that this was a permanently running section, with the identification of potential new markets for its services as just one of its allotted tasks. The TSG had submitted a report to the BTC at some time prior to 26th July 1956 in

Facing page: It was the luxury travel market that the trains were intended to capture, and it must be said that in this they were very successful for a number of years. This shot of a customer having sugar added to his melon is staged, as many of the pre-public service shots showing the on-train catering were posed using railway staff from the various Public Relations and Press Office departments. Even so, it made for good advertising as well as giving the waiters some practice if required. (It is believed the train staff was exclusively male, for no other reason than the fact that equivalent butler-type roles were still predominantly male-orientated at the time.) The handle for adjusting the blinds can be seen, just where a tall passenger could strike his head on it. In first-class the blinds had a tendency to stick at a drunken angle, which did little to promote the luxury image; they would also rattle against the glass of the windows on occasions. Notice one of the table lamps, which were the subject of much discussion later (see pages 11 and 12); perhaps they too give the appearance of being an afterthought. (As an aside, one train steward had a party trick of being able to whip the tablecloth away from the table without bringing the crockery and glasses crashing down, although the fact that the table linen was of a very silky texture no doubt helped him achieve this.) (BR/LMR Public Relations and Press Office)

which it concluded that the railway should provide three distinct types of express passenger service in future.

The first of these was a Pullman de-luxe service, intended for the business traveller for which a supplementary fare would be charged. Next were special express services, limited in capacity, and again with the possibility of a supplementary charge. Finally there were the ordinary express services. Pullman services were deemed to be strictly in the first category. Interestingly, three individuals who were involved in the subsequent discussion on the points raised by the TSG also sat on the Phillips Committee. It might be said that the BTC set its own set agenda as to the conclusions it wished to see reached, and (purely the opinion of the present writer) adopted the principle that "if you don't like the result, move the goalposts!" (Surviving paperwork reveals the decline in passenger journeys that was occurring at the time. From a peak of 1.295 million journeys in 1937, it had shrunk to 1.001 million in 1951 and to 0.991 million by 1954. At the same time the number of vehicles on the roads had doubled. One rather strange figure was that in 1954 there had been 1,002,000 domestic air passengers in the UK as well.)

The choice of Leeds as a potential terminus for the new service has already been mentioned, and it is appropriate to state that the reluctance of the Committee to recommend the Yorkshire city for the new trains was based on potentially sound logic. The Modernisation Plan envisaged early electrification of the East Coast Main Line, which implied a major engineering upheaval roughly coinciding with the introduction of the new trains. Even at this stage the BTC was very conscious of its public image, and wisely felt that a prestige new service affected by major delay was far from advisable. (As it transpired electrification of the ECML was delayed, and steam was eventually superseded by the Deltic diesels; the route was not electrified until many years later.)

According to Charles Long, the BTC made the decision to market the new trains as Pullman services in July 1956, and although no specific date is known for the decision, it is safe to say that it was subsequent to the submission of the two reports outlined above. From the Phillips Committee, the BTC distilled the technical details and the make-up of the trains, while it was the views of the Traffic Survey Group that determined the standard of service to be provided. Perhaps this proves that the criteria that the Committee had been working to had indeed been altered at some stage, but the BTC's decision was to have far-reaching consequences, and would also lead to a difficult relationship between its own catering arm and the newly-acquired Pullman company.

Charles Long again makes an interesting comment on the whole Pullman concept, now that the decision had been made to market the proposed new trains under that name. As mentioned previously, the Committee had set out its idea of the proposed train layout (both six- and eight-car) which, while it included two kitchen cars, adopted a "2+1" seating arrangement for first class. Possibly some of the die-hards of the Pullman Car Co regret-

ted this break away from the traditional "1+1" seating, but had this been adopted in the new trains, the total accommodation in a six-car set would have been no more than 88 passengers. (It would also have increased the passenger ticket price by a proportionate amount, which would already have been set at the equivalent cost of a single air ticket between Manchester and London.)

With the decision made to produce the new trains to the Pullman standard, the Committee made the understandable recommendation to the BTC that the work should be entrusted to Wolverton Carriage Works, with the exception of the power cars where, to avoid any delay caused by tendering, a suitable firm should be selected in conjunction with the Carriage & Wagon Builders Association, "subject to adequate financial safeguards", which together would ensure the quickest delivery time. However, an additional difficulty was that, as the vehicles were to carry the Pullman name, BR workshops could not legally produce them, as Pullman was still deemed to be an outside company. Accordingly all the work had to be entrusted to a contractor.

On 29th November 1956, the BTC accepted an estimate of £1,215,000 from Metropolitan-Cammell to cover the design and construction of the 36 vehicles that would form the five train sets. Two would consist of six-cars, and the other three of eight cars. The estimate quoted included the necessary sub-contractor work that would involve the supply of the power units and other ancillary equipment. The contract for construction was signed on 14th December of the same year.

It was decided that the two six-car sets would operate on the LMR between Manchester and London, David Blee, the General Manager of the region, having confirmed this in a memorandum to the BTC on 22nd October 1956. His note stated that, "the decision to serve Manchester has been influenced by the concern at the growing increase in air travel between the city and London, and it is considered most desirable to provide a competitive alternative…by the introduction of a high-speed service with exceptional standards of comfort, catering and service". Even so, Blee voiced what would later be a oft-quoted criticism that it would be necessary to maintain one train as a spare, but that, "the practicalities of obtaining additional mileage by running intermediate services between London and Leicester is being examined". Presumably there would also have been a similar commitment by the management of the Western Region around the same time, but evidence for this has not been located. (In 1956, there was a brief discussion about making all the trains consist of eight cars.)

The question of a spare train-set is interesting. The Committee had identified a need for one in its July 1956 report, with paragraphs 4.4 and 4.5 accepting that, the requirement for "one spare train set for each region is high…if further sets are introduced then this will reduce." There was no mention of the necessity to maintain locomotive-hauled cars as stand-bys, as was done later.

Nowhere does it appear to have been considered that perhaps a half train-set would have sufficed as a spare, as was the arrangement with the TEE sets. As already mentioned, the initial proposals for the new Pullman sets showed each half-set to be a mirror of the other, and it was later the practice to split the trains in two when necessary. Although this would have been the most economic proposition, financial constraints do not appear to have been the driving influence at this stage, although there was a comment from the BTC that the quoted cost for the inclusion of air conditioning was too high, and there was therefore a definite risk that this feature might be omitted. Fortunately, that was not the case and air-conditioning was to become one of the strongest selling points of the new service.

The concept was announced to the public with some speed almost as soon as the agreement for construction had been arranged: "As part of the Modernisation Plan announced last year, British Railways are to introduce a new high-speed Diesel Multiple Unit built to operate between important cities, and to contain all that is the best to offer for the comfort and amenity of the passenger. Public reaction to the new trains will be carefully watched before increasing the fleet." Possibly to keep matters in

the public eye, a further announcement was made in March 1957, in which it was stated that it was hoped to introduce the trains in March 1958; it must have been obvious to the hierarchy of BR at that time that this was somewhat optimistic. Colin Marsden in his excellent publication *Modern Railways Profile No 10*, refers to tenders being sought in 1958/9, but in truth, there was no way the trains could have been ready in time if this was correct.

All that was left now was to turn an approved concept into reality. The fact that this took less than three years was quite commendable bearing in mind the complexities involved. The main difficulty was that the social scene and expectations of the travelling public were moving on at an ever-increasing pace as the end of the decade approached. Had the new trains arrived earlier, they might have had a greater acceptance, but although it was expected that there would be a book life of 30 years in which to recoup the investment, no-one could have foreseen the changes in lifestyle and expectations that would occur within only a third of that time.

The new Pullman crest (perhaps more accurately described as a Coat of Arms) that was applied to both the front and sides of the new trains. This item is discussed in detail in Chapter 4.

Part of a mock-up of the design, believed to be a section of the wooden model referred to in this chapter. The headcode panel is a feature that was not perpetuated in the production vehicles, yet its inclusion was still being considered in 1958. The wording on the side is also interesting.

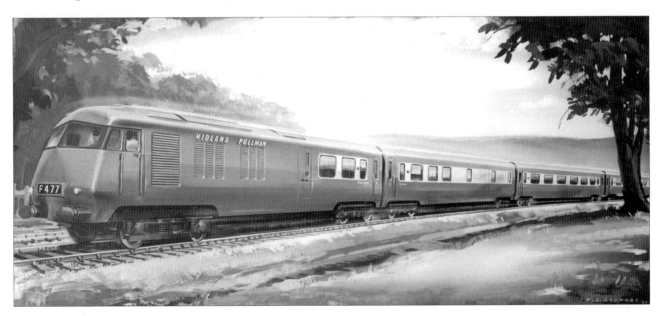

This 1957 artist's impression was broadly similar to the units as they eventually appeared. The route-indicator panel has been mentioned, but also note the dark colouring around the cab windows. The lack of detail below the solebar is understandable at this stage, but it can also be seen that the window spacing of the power car is closer to what was later used for the WR sets.

(BR/LMR Public Relations and Press Office)

Chapter 2

FROM CONCEPT TO REALITY

Metropolitan-Cammell and its sub-contractors lost no time in developing the new trains, but it was not to be a straightforward process. It has been suggested that the BTC's comment over the cost of the air-conditioning might have led whole project being abandoned on cost grounds. How close this was to the truth will never be known, but cost in other areas would raise its head later.

The potential threat from the proposed motorway network, allied to the ongoing development of internal air services, principally operated by British European Airways (BEA), appeared to be enough to convince the BTC, not only of the need for the new trains, but also for as much haste as possible in their design and development. It would be tempting to think that because of the imaginative nature of the design, just Metropolitan-Cammell and BR were involved, but this is not known for certain. Instead, it appears that the sub-contractors were almost given a free hand from the outset, although naturally not without due consultation. Metropolitan-Cammell was a firm whose roots went back to the previous century, and who were a most respected railway engineering company. BR was also fully stretched with the design and development of new traction generally, but in one area at least, there was cross-communication, and this was with the Design Panel, which had been established by the BTC in 1956.

It is relevant at this stage look into the rationale behind the setting up of the Design Panel, which was intended to portray a modern and progressive image to the public. Part of the rationale was a justifiable fear that locomotives and multiple units could present a bland, perhaps even stark appearance, and with the future success of the railway generally perceived to be related as much to image as to accounts, steps were considered necessary to present an appropriate face to the world. The Design Panel can be considered as the first step towards the evolution of BR's Modern Image, but with much design work on locomotives and rolling stock out of BR's hands, there was a genuine risk that certain manufacturers and their in-house designers could have too much of a free rein. The reaction to this was the potential stifling of ideas, although the remit of the Design Panel was actually more towards aesthetics than engineering.

Beauty is in the eye of the beholder, of course, and while this is not the time to discuss the relative aesthetics of the first fleet of diesels (for which the reader is referred to Brian Haresnape's *British Rail 1948-1978, a Journey by Design*) it cannot be disputed that the appearance of some of the first-generation locomotives and multiple units was, frankly, appalling.

All credit, therefore, to BR for identifying this at an early stage, but it must also be said that the Design Panel was hampered by limited staff resources, as well as a reluctance, sometimes even hostility, from manufacturers to effect change. Haresnape expounds on this well in

his book, and the result was that machines introduced after 1956 did not always benefit from aesthetic advantages that might otherwise have been gained. (A classic example from the negative end of the spectrum is the Metro-Vick Co-Bo design of 1958, while at the opposite end, the Western class from 1961 was one of the best looking diesel types ever.)

For the Blue Pullman project, BR appointed Jack Howe, FRIBA, FSIA, as a design consultant. The aesthetic theme was given added importance by the BTC's appointment of George Williams as Design Officer for the Panel. (Jack Howe would later have some input into the design of the Mark 2 locomotive-hauled Pullman coaches of the 1960s.)

Unfortunately, Jack Howe's enthusiasm was not universally shared by all of the Pullman Car Company's senior managers. Charles Long commented that the non-traditional approach that Howe brought with him was unwelcome and would be resisted from the start. But to be fair, much of this was based on the change from pre-war Pullman ideals and service levels to what would nowadays be called "blue-sky thinking", where nothing was sacrosanct. An example of this was the insistence by the Pullman management that table lamps be provided. These were totally unnecessary, as the diffused lighting in the new vehicles was more than sufficient. However, Pullman had always had separate lamps for each table, and it was their will that eventually prevailed. (The term "table-lamp" is used for simplicity, but is strictly inaccurate in this context, as the lamps were attached by a swan-neck stem to the interior waist panelling of the vehicle, rather than being attached directly to the tables.) Jack Howe was seemingly so incensed over their inclusion that on 17th June 1959, he wrote to George Williams on the subject,

"I am enclosing for your information a copy of a drawing number 134/40 showing details of the proposed Pullman table lamp. You are, I know, aware that I have produced this design under protest because I consider it entirely unnecessary, and in my opinion it detracts from the overall design of the coaches. I take a very poor view indeed of *(the Chairman of Pullman)* Sir John Elliot's action in demanding these lamps at a time when all the details of the train interior had been approved by the Design Panel and the Pullman Car Company.

"As you know, structural changes had to be made and wiring rerouted in order to accommodate them, and I would say that this change alone has unnecessarily added at least £5,000 to the cost of the job. In view of *(the CME of BR)* Mr Harrisons's urgent plea for economy, I think this is a shocking waste of money. As Mr Summerson *(a member of the Design Panel)* was present when the final prototype interiors were approved, and he himself came out strongly against table lamps, I would like him to know my views on the matter."

A typically 1960s publicity view, clearly showing one of "those" table lamps. Elsewhere the table cloth, ash tray, and antimacassar were all to the unique design specified for the new trains.

(Antony M Ford Collection)

Strong words indeed, and Howe's argument was one that could hardly be disputed on financial grounds. Perhaps with hindsight, Elliot can be seen to have been correct, but only on the basis of aesthetics, and all of the trains were ultimately equipped with table lamps. In other areas, the ideas of the designers (not necessarily the Design Panel) were also found to be too radical. One was that the addition of air-conditioning would remove the need to segregate smoking and non-smoking passengers; in practice, this did not work.

An amusing sideline, was the perfectly logical suggestion that toilets should be segregated for ladies and gentlemen. Accordingly, the panelling in those intended for female use was pink, and that for males, blue, although the fittings in each cubicle were identical. While, in theory, this was a perfectly sound suggestion, the percentage of female passengers could not be guaranteed to be very high, so to avoid a potentially long walk to find an unoccupied cubicle, the idea was abandoned before the trains entered service, although the colour of the panelling, blue or pink, confirmed the original intention.

On a more serious note, the design of the new trains demanded a radically new type of bogie, and following a, reportedly, extensive search, the Swiss Schlierien design was selected. (Aspects of this were later modified by Metropolitan-Cammell to suit the new trains, and the product fitted under the Blue Pullmans was then formally known as the Metro-Schlieren bogie.) Wisely, a number of these bogies were given extensive testing in their original form under three standard Mark1 vehicles operating on the LMR in 1958, where they apparently gave excellent results. It would be appropriate at this time to include details of these tests, but unfortunately a report has not been located. (Tests involving other types of bogie were being undertaken under various Mark 1 coaches around this period as well.)

Little else has come to light relating to the construction of the trains at the Metropolitan-Cammell works during the period December 1956 through to October 1959. No doubt much correspondence was exchanged, but although the Metropolitan-Cammell archive has passed to a respected research body, it is unfortunately inaccessible, and is likely to remain so for the foreseeable future.

This is almost the only gap in the history of the trains, and moving ahead to the autumn of 1959, official records reveal delivery times starting in September 1959 for the first of the LMR 6-car sets with the second LMR train being completed the next month. Consecutive months then saw the three 8-car WR sets being delivered

Posed in works grey within the yard of the builders, Metropolitan-Cammell, this is the front end of one of the LMR power cars, later numbered in the series M60090-3.

(Metropolitan-Cammell/Kidderminster Railway Museum)

until the last of the trains was completed by the builders in January 1960.

At this stage, the true costs were reported, and came to a total of £1,662,000 against the original estimate of £1,215,000, an increase of nearly 37%, which does not take inflation into account. A 6-car train was reported as costing £285,000 and an 8-car train, £341,500. Spares accounted for a further £57,500, and there is also an entry for "Special Design" costs amounting to £10,000, half of which was possibly attributable to those table lamps! These figures do not appear to include any allowance for the provision of the necessary fixed installations, such as maintenance sheds and shore supplies. (These items are discussed in the chapters dealing with the running and operation of the trains on the LMR and WR.) Elsewhere, contemporary correspondence refers to a higher total figure of £1,998,002, but this does includes a reference to spares.

The overall influence of Jack Howe was considerable, and it was he who had especially arranged for the uncluttered appearance of the front end of the trains, including the removal of the 4-character head-code panel that had been proposed. The result was a streamlined

train, the like of which had never been seen before in Britain, and which was justifiably presented as the prestige symbol of the Modernisation Plan - the British counterpart to the European Trans-Europe Express services.

The whole train was packed with innovative ideas and luxury features, and notwithstanding the fact that it was Pullman-only, it was still a considerable advance on anything seen previously. (The counter argument could be that before WWII, the LMS and the LNER had run, respectively, the Coronation Scot and Coronation services, but while these services easily eclipsed the regular workings of the 1950s, they did not approach the unashamed luxury that the Blue Pullman offered. The only other contender would be the GWR's single train of Super Saloons, but these were used solely on very special workings and were not available to the general public. Nor were any of these trains fully air-conditioned, as was the Blue Pullman.)

Apart from the mechanics, which are discussed later, the body sides were smooth and clean in detail. Perhaps the least satisfactory features, from a visual perspective, were the gaps between the car and the exposed jumper cables. While both could have been improved

The same vehicle as on the previous page, but photographed side on. This series of photographs is undated but was probably taken around the summer of 1959. While the body sides and ends have clearly yet to be painted, other parts of the final livery have been applied, such as the light grey roof, aluminium underframe and black bogies. The surrounds to the headlamps incorporated a simple frame into which either a red filter or blanking plate could be slotted.

(Metropolitan-Cammell/Kidderminster Railway Museum)

Two completed LMR power cars at Saltley. The provision of just two warning horns will be noted. All the sets were gradually fitted with an additional warning horn on the right-hand side looking from the front. Additionally, the cover over the coupling housing appears at this stage to be solid and not slotted. The material used for the front end was metal, not plastic as on the later HSTs, and the design ran to no less than 13 mock-ups, which were produced by the builder in various sizes before the final front-end design was approved.

(Metropolitan-Cammell/Kidderminster Railway Museum)

upon, there were to be no changes throughout the life of the trains. But this criticism only applies to the external look of the train, for internally, there was a vast improvement on the design for the internal gangways. Long regarded as one of the worst features of the traditional railway carriage, and invariably dark, draughty and dirty, there was now a clean, wide passage, mounted on pivots at each carriage end, which formed a semi-floating, rubber-sealed platform, that also prevented any loss of air-conditioning. Indeed, the passenger scarcely noticed the transition from one car to the next.

Moving to the interior proper, the passenger doors were designed to open inwards in standard Pullman style, and were provided at the ends only, the early suggestion for centre doors having been abandoned. Inside the traditional Edwardian Pullman, with its timber panelling and marquetry, was consigned to history. Instead, first-class passengers were regaled with grey leathercloth walls, set off by either ebony or polished rosewood partitions, the

partitions having inlaid murals by William Mitchell. (The style of panelling was one of the few vestiges of traditional Pullman styling.) (Other reports refer to a George Mitchell being responsible, whose work graced the London Barbican and the Co-Operative building in Manchester). Carpet colours were radical and varied, being red and black or blue and black. Seats were fully adjustable and reclinable. (For more detail on which colours were installed, and where, see Chapter 4.)

Second class on the WR sets was not forgotten either, although here, the use of modern materials saw a grey plastic used for the partitions, again with the same comfortable seating. It was only on the sets destined for the WR that some form of differentiation in seating was provided, as on these trains, the second class had fixed, (as opposed to adjustable) "aircraft-style" seats. Wide windows, similar to that on the Cravens prototype coach of 1957, were a feature of the design, and were double-glazed with adjustable passenger-operated Venetian

This and facing page: Side views of WR power car W60099, numerically the last of the type, but not necessarily the last to be built. Note the car identification lettering, this vehicle being "H". The date of the views is not known, but it is reasonable to assume that they were taken fairly early on. The reference on the side destination blind on one of the vehicles to "Bristol Pullman – Bath Spa, Chippenham, and Paddington" is interesting, as this was not the itinerary originally worked in 1960 (see Chapter 6). There are some perspective lines drawn by the artist on the view showing the left-hand side of the car, and these were no doubt then transferred for use on a poster or other form of advertising. These two views were amongst those that started the author on the quest for the Blue Pullman story, having been purchased for a paltry few pounds at an exhibition.

blinds. (The Cravens coach was one of several built in the 1950s as prototypes for quantity production to follow on from the BR Mark1 vehicles, and it too featured blinds of the type described. Unfortunately BR considered the vehicle too luxurious, and consequently too expensive, although quantity production would undoubtedly have reduced the cost. In many ways the Cravens vehicle was years ahead of its time, and was superior in design to what later became the Standard Mark 2 vehicle of the 1960s.)

So much innovation had gone into the Blue Pullman trains, which in external design alone, typified all that was best in contemporary engineering, that it was not surprising that the cover of the August 1960 issue of *Design*, the journal of industrial design, featured a colour illustration of the new trains. Additionally, Messrs Stones (the sub-contractor responsible for the air-conditioning, as well as some other components) produced their own booklet featuring the train in order to promote their own involvement. The undoubted modernity of the project meant that companies were justifiably proud to be associated with it. (Until the mid 1960s, Stones had a virtual monopoly in the supply of air-conditioning equipment to BR, and according to Michael Harris in his book, *British Rail Mark 2 Coaches*, it was a monopoly BR was keen to break.)

Perhaps the greatest benefit for the passengers, regardless of their class of travel, was the air conditioning, which was fitted for the first time to a production train in the UK. In this respect, the new units scored far better than anything that had gone before, but to be strictly accurate, what was fitted was what would now be referred to as climate-control, rather than air-conditioning.

As befitted the prestige train of BR, the attention to detail was staggering, and again showed the hand of Jack Howe. It included lighting by diffused fluorescent tubes, carriage litter bins, magazine trays, instruction leaflets for the adjustable seating, antimacassars, a new range of sil-

ver plate and glassware with modernized Pullman insignia, signs and notices, all in a more modern Pullman style, and a mosaic wall in the toilets, the internal finish of which were exceptionally well designed and featured passenger controlled water temperature delivered to a capacious wash basin by a single spray nozzle. Finishing off the passenger detailing was a public address system, known as the "Loudaphone" system, the loudspeakers for which were concealed above the luggage racks on one side of the ceiling. Communication was possible between the Guard or Conductor and the passengers, or between the Guard and the Driver on a separate circuit. Instructions were given to staff to keep public announcements to a minimum, and if possible, to restrict them to advice about arrival points. (The detailed preparation that went into service was considerable. Suggestions were even given for the wording to be used when making announcements. One example for the up Midland Pullman was, "Good morning Ladies and Gentlemen, welcome to the Blue Pullman. In a few minutes we shall stop at Cheadle Heath to take on more passengers, after which breakfast will be served.")

Despite the new image, traditional Pullman standards of service were maintained, with a push-button and indicator light to summon the attendant to an individual table. Part of the appeal of the new trains was, undoubtedly, the striking colour scheme of Nanking blue bodywork with white window surrounds. This was surmounted by a specially redesigned Pullman coat of arms, and shaded, Egyptian slab-serif lettering, the whole very different from the traditional umber associated with Pullman vehicles up until that time. As first built, the white colour applied to the window surrounds did not run the full length of the train, but a break occurred on the side of the kitchen cars where there were no windows. This spoilt the otherwise aesthetic lines of the trains, and prompted another letter from Jack Howe to George Wil-

liams. Dated 17th February 1960, it was less caustic than his previous letter:

"I have heard rumours that the Pullman trains will not be put into service on the Midland Region until June. I believe they are passing backwards and forwards between Metropolitan-Cammell and British Railways, and I wondered whether you could bring some pressure to bear at your end for the exterior painting on the kitchen cars to be completed as designed. You will remember that this was not done, and there was a gap in the white band at each end which we agreed was not happy."

So far, a relatively mild and justified comment, but the second and final paragraph of his letter sees Howe far more determined:

"Metropolitan-Cammell who, at the time I brought the matter up, were under considerable pressure from BTC to complete the first two trains, obstinately refused to do anything about it, but now we seem to have a bit of extra time, I think it would be a pity if they went into service in their present state."

How this change to the paintwork was subsequently achieved is irrelevant. But Howe's wishes prevailed, and all the trains entered public service with the white band running the full length of the windows. The significance of this change has not always been obvious to previous commentators, and means that views showing a break in the white band can only have been taken before July 1960. In turn, photographs of services operating in the incomplete livery cannot have been revenue-earning

turns, and both the LMR and WR sets entered service with the same uniform colour scheme throughout the length of the sets. One area over which there does not appear to have been any dispute was the carrying of names, and there was never a suggestion that the first class vehicles should do so.

The second paragraph of Howe's letter also implies some friction between the builders and the BTC, but this cannot be elaborated upon as, to date, no correspondence from this period has been located.

None of this is in any way intended to imply criticism of the builders, indeed with the initial planning complete, it is to the credit of Metropolitan-Cammell that they were able to achieve so much in such a short space of time. This included a full-size mock up of part of a car, which was displayed to the senior staff of the LMR, the WR and the Pullman Car Co. Their reaction is not formally reported, but it was almost certainly positive, and might have triggered Sir John Elliot's insistence on the provision of table lamps. At some stage, another wooden mock-up was made of the whole train, this time to a scale of half an inch to a foot, which amounted to something just over 16½ft for a six-car set. Various reports in recent years have suggested that at one stage this was on display at the public school at either Repton or Rugby, but the reason for either of these strange resting places is not known. Like the full-size mock-up, its subsequent fate is not recorded, and was presumably destroyed.

1 Condenser	13 Luggage	25 Table lamps	37 Radiator air intake
2 Contactor switch box	14 Rubber tread	26 Loudspeakers in ceiling	38 Engine air intake
3 24-V. battery	15 Control panel	27 Locker	39 Generator air intake
4 Fuel tank filler both sides	16 Filter chamber	28 H.T. cubicle	40 Reservoir
5 Alternator	17 Fuse and linen cupboard	29 L.T. cubicle	41 Exhaust pipe
6 Air filter	18 Refrigerator	30 Microphone	42 Double glazed windows, venetian blind between
7 Auxiliary engine	19 Floor drain	31 Fire extinguisher	
8 Radiator	20 Steriliser	32 Bracket for A.T.C. receiver	43 Instruments
9 E.P. brake unit	21 Sink	33 Motor air intake	44 Vent-Axia fan
10 Gas cylinders	22 Gas range with fume chamber over	34 Air conditioning intake and filters	45 Service indicator box
11 Radiator header tank filler			
12 Air conditioning exhaust and air intake filter on opposite sides	23 Silencer	35 Air conditioning exhaust	
	24 Tank filler	36 Radiator exhaust fan	

Key to diagrams on pages 19, 20 and 21.

BRITISH TRANSPORT COMMISSION
PULLMAN DE LUXE HIGH SPEED TRAINS
WITH METRO-SCHLIEREN BOGIES
POWER CAR TYPE P.1
LOT NO. 30553
Length over Body   66' 5.1/2"   Centre of Bogies   46' 6"
Length over Buffers 68' 6.1/2"   Bogie Wheelbase   9' 6"
Width over Panels   9' 0"   Tare Weight   67.24 Tons
Built by
METROPOLITAN-CAMMELL CARRIAGE & WAGON CO. LTD.,
ENGLAND
1960

NO.18870   NEG. NO. 9127

Another official view, clearly taken at a later date in view of the general workaday grime that is apparent. It could be that this record was made at the time of one of the bogie modifications, judging by the smudged chalk marks on the rear bogie. The guards/luggage compartment has the obligatory notice "Load 15 cwts distributed".
(Metropolitan-Cammell/Kidderminster Railway Museum)

On the following pages are various plans reproduced to a scale of 4mm to 1ft. Page 19 shows the elevation of a power car with alternative layout for LMR (type 1) and WR (type 2) cars. Page 20 shows the elevation and plan for a type 3 parlour car as used on the WR 8-car sets. Also on this page is a kitchen car elevation. On page 21 are two variations of internal layout for kitchen cars and a further parlour car layout. A key to the numbering on these diagrams is included on page 17, and the make up of the LMR 6-car and WR 8-car trains is shown below.
(Courtesy, "The Railway Gazette", ref issues of 14th June, 1st July and 8th July, 1960)

MOTOR CAR TYPE 2	PARLOUR CAR TYPE 3	KITCHEN CAR TYPE 5	PARLOUR CAR TYPE 5	KITCHEN CAR TYPE 5	PARLOUR CAR TYPE 6	PARLOUR CAR TYPE 6	KITCHEN CAR TYPE 5	PARLOUR CAR TYPE 5	PARLOUR CAR TYPE 3	MOTOR CAR TYPE 2

---- 545' 1" LENGTH OVER BUFFERS ----

MOTOR CAR TYPE 1	KITCHEN CAR TYPE 4	PARLOUR CAR TYPE 6	PARLOUR CAR TYPE 6	KITCHEN CAR TYPE 4	MOTOR CAR TYPE 1

---- 409' 1" LENGTH OVER BUFFERS ----

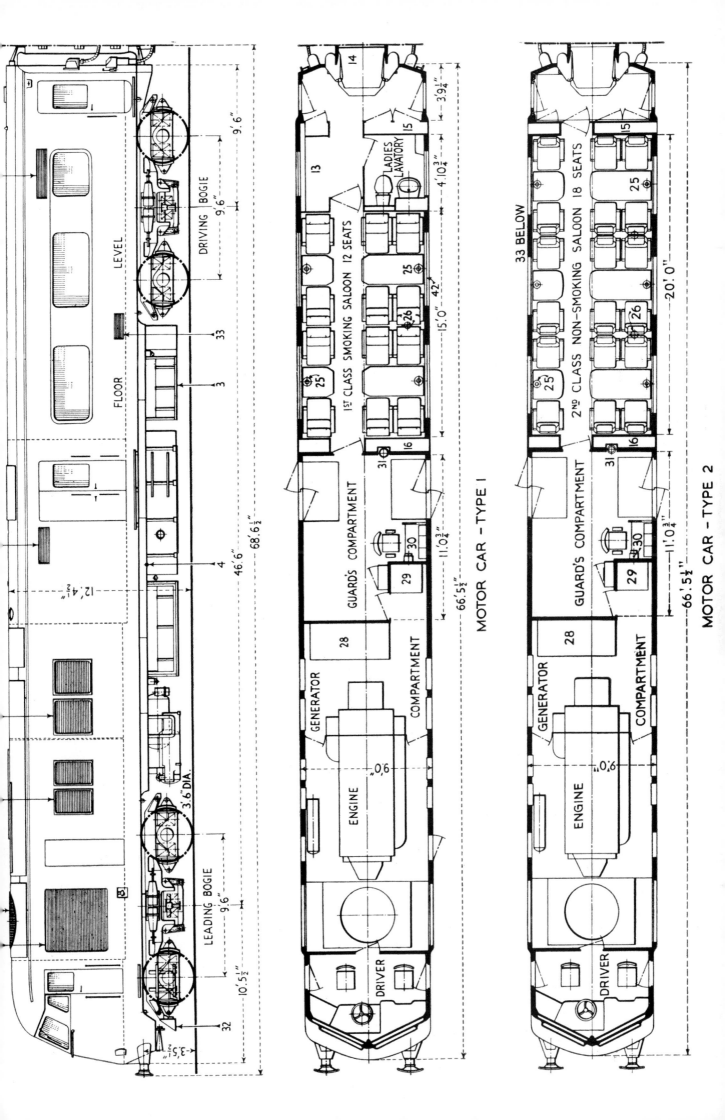

9'6"

LEVEL

DRIVING BOGIE

9'6"

FLOOR

33

3

4

12'4½"

68'6½"

46'6"

3'6" DIA.

LEADING BOGIE

9'6"

10'5½"

32

3'5½"

14

13

LADIES LAVATORY

15

3'9¼"

4'10¾"

42'

15'0"

25

26

25

1ST CLASS SMOKING SALOON 12 SEATS

16

31

GUARD'S COMPARTMENT

66'5½"

11'0¾"

30

29

28

GENERATOR

COMPARTMENT

ENGINE

6'0"

DRIVER

MOTOR CAR – TYPE 1

33 BELOW

15

25

26

25

2ND CLASS NON-SMOKING SALOON 18 SEATS

20'0"

16

31

GUARD'S COMPARTMENT

11'0¾"

66'5½"

30

29

28

GENERATOR

COMPARTMENT

ENGINE

6'0"

DRIVER

MOTOR CAR – TYPE 2

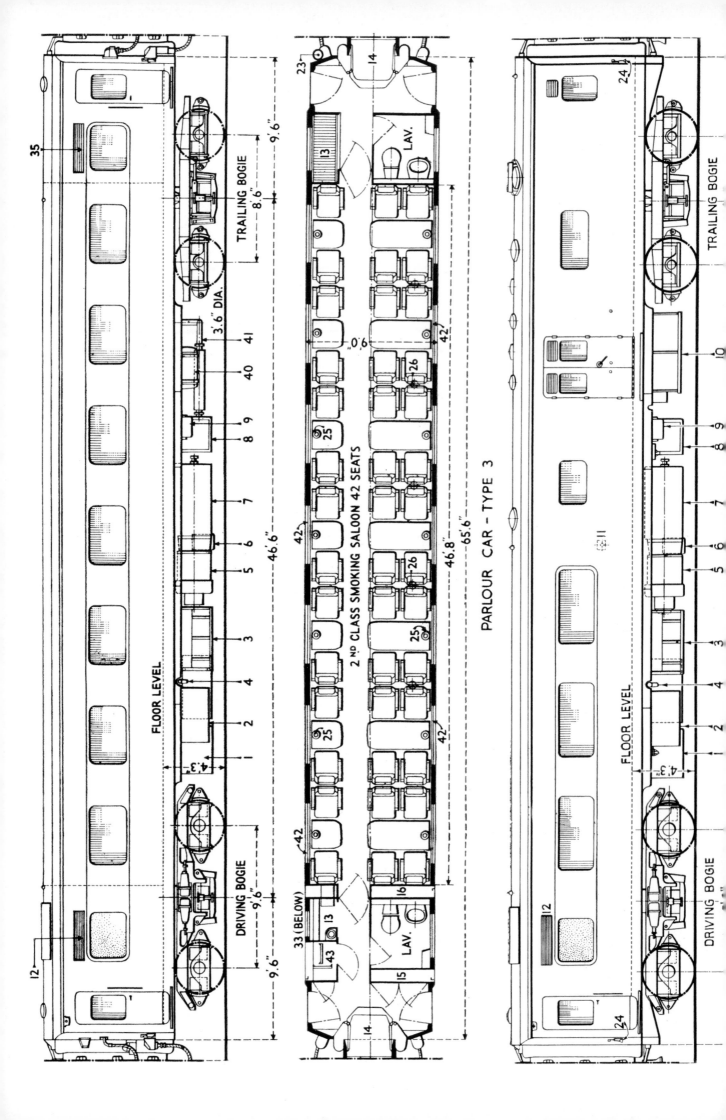

2ND CLASS SMOKING SALOON 42 SEATS

PARLOUR CAR - TYPE 3

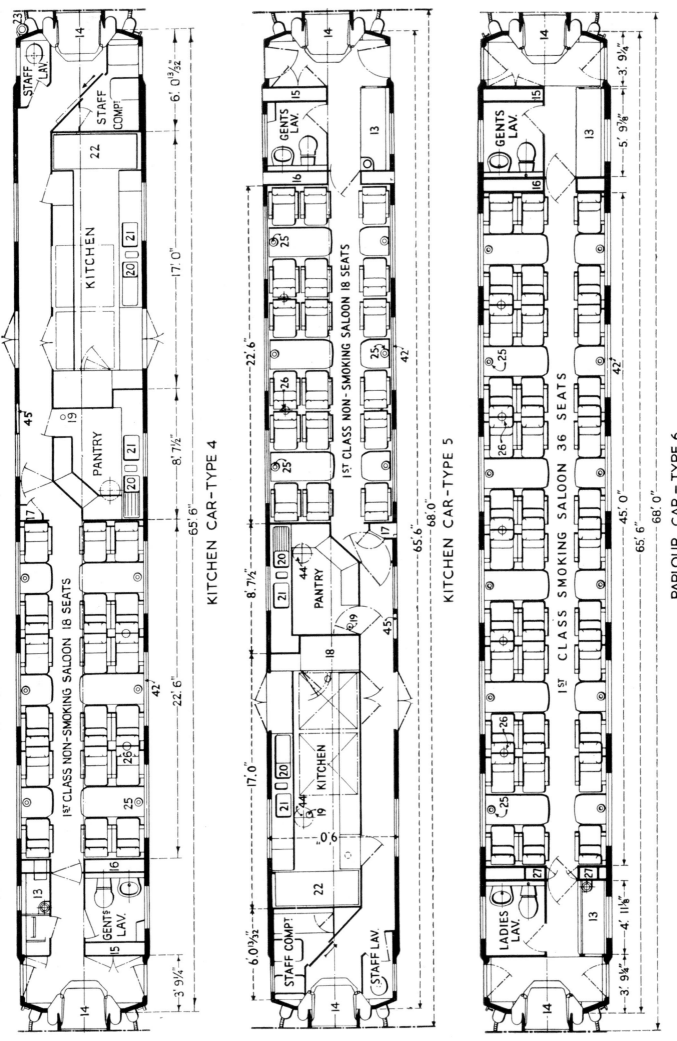

KITCHEN CAR – TYPE 4

KITCHEN CAR – TYPE 5

PARLOUR CAR – TYPE 6

Chapter 3

TESTING, PUBLICITY AND INTO SERVICE

A public announcement about the introduction of the new trains was made by BR in March 1957, and with an expected start date sometime in 1958. Clearly, this was somewhat optimistic for what was, after all, a totally new venture, and the fact that the full order for 36 vehicles was eventually completed in less than 42 months was a remarkable achievement.

The first complete 6-car train-set (at this stage referred to as 60091, 60731, 60741, 60740, 60730, and 60090, although Mxxxx series numbers were used later), was out-shopped from Saltley in September 1959, although prior to this, it is believed that the first two motor coaches had been tested separately within the works area. It was reported that trial running of a complete set commenced on 18th October 1959, so presumably the set was

involved in static tests and slow speed maneuvering within the makers yard between those dates. On BR, the first runs were from the Metropolitan-Cammell works at Saltley as far as Lichfield Road Junction near Walsall. This took the units north of Birmingham through Castle Bromwich and Aldridge, a distance of almost 31 miles. The trials were not confined to weekdays, and line occupancy resulted in a number of runs being made at weekends, with at least one on a Sunday during the autumn. The sets destined for the Western Region were tried out in the same fashion.

Some time later in October, the first set moved to Derby where it would be based for test running over the Midland main line. The second train later joined it there, and although no date for this is given, completion of this

Above: Local trials around Birmingham with WR W60096 at Aldridge; the third air horn has been added by now and a draw hook for emergency coupling was installed behind the round casing between the buffers. Despite the blue livery, the buffer shanks at the front end of all the power cars (LMR and WR) were painted red.

Facing page: M66091, this time and with the plain door instead. The location is Lichfield Road Junction on Sunday 18th October 1959, with the set having just completed a trial run from Saltley. The number of people travelling will also be noted. At this stage, the Pullman crest has yet to be added to the front of the power car. (Richard HF Moore)

set was during October 1959, which points to it being transferred to Derby in the November. Around this time a number of publicity photographs were taken on the Wirksworth branch, a favorite location for such events. Moving ahead slightly, it is appropriate to mention that similar photographic shoots are known to have taken place in March 1960 on the Bedford-Hitchin branch. In addition, the former Midland Railway line from Kettering towards Cambridge was used for slow speed stop-start testing.

Main line running began in mid-November 1959, the first run taking place on the Midland line between Leicester and Luton, on 16th November 1959. The original 6-car set ran in a 'Q' path (these were spare paths available in the timetable for extra or special workings, which could then be slotted in without interfering with other traffic), behind the 8.55am Manchester Central to St Pancras, and returned from Luton behind the 12.25pm St Pancras to Manchester Central. This was also the official date that the first was formally handed over to BR "for testing, staff training and familiarisation", and it was from this time that the well-known difficulties over the riding quality began to be noted. This is not unduly surprising, as prior to this date any trials would have been at lower speeds.

A Press Day was also provisionally scheduled for sometime in November 1959 with the intended introduction of the new service from 4th January 1960 – although other reports refer to 11th January. Without doubt this was somewhat optimistic as there is reference in surviving paperwork to "teething difficulties" and even more poignantly, "technical difficulties". In the event any launch was first put back to March and then July. There was also seemingly no response from the Press over any of these cancellations or delays so it is likely that the dates quoted were "targets" only. Possibly to cover themselves though, a memorandum was prepared in which a useful covering, but also truthful statement was made. It referred to the month of January as being a bad month in which to introduce any new service as weather delays were more likely to occur at that time of year.

The main-line trials involved various tests including emergency brake tests, which showed that on a falling gradient of 1 in 200, a 6-car train could come to a stop from 90mph in 1,202 yards in a time of 53.8 seconds. At 45mph, the time was just 16.5 seconds in a distance of 206 yards. The weather and rail conditions during the trials were not reported, but the information gained assisted the calculation of accurate scheduling and permissible maximum speeds over varying sections of line. Due allowance had to be made for braking distances in what was almost entirely a mechanically signalled area. High-speed running tests were also undertaken around this time.

Before the appearance of the first diesel sets, the LMR had embarked on at least one high-speed steam trial between Manchester and St. Pancras. This took place on 25th August 1959, and involved a Jubilee and just three coaches, one of which was the track-recording car. The run was completed in 3 hours 15 minutes, but that did include a severe loss of time due to a permanent way slack. (The Pullman service would later be scheduled at 3 hours 10 minutes.) It is possible that this trial was to establish whether a substitute steam service might be viable, if required.

An interesting and important operational procedure was double-block working, where a train could not be accepted by a signalman unless, not only was his block clear to the next box, but also that of the box ahead. In this way faster speeds could be maintained, but the trade off was the difficulty in keeping other traffic out of the way. Double-block working had been used by the LNER in pre-war days for its streamlined express workings. Whether the double-block working on the LMR applied to just the high-speed steam trial mentioned, the test runs of the Blue Pullman, or even the normal public service (and if so, for how long), is not clear. (By comparison, double-block working was never adopted by the WR.)

The Midland line between St. Pancras and Manchester was not fitted with Automatic Train Control (ATC), so the trains destined for the LMR were not equipped with the necessary cab equipment (although brackets for the later addition of this equipment were provided). The omission of ATC from the new LMR trains, together with the intention to run a regular fast service over a congested route, is curious. True, the equipping of the whole route between St Pancras and Manchester with ATC would have been very expensive, but it also seems that certain elements within BR had short memories after the terrible collision at Harrow and Wealdstone, just a few years earlier in 1952. Here, the provision of ATC might have prevented a terrible loss of life, and the accident was followed by BR publicly announcing that they intended to equip all main lines with train protection as soon as possible. Yet just eight years later, a faster service than had ever existed before on the Midland main line was introduced on where ATC was conspicuous by its absence. Readers must form their own opinions on the decisions made at the time. By contrast, on the WR, the lines out of Paddington to both Bristol and Birmingham had long been fitted with the GWR-style ATC contact ramps, and the WR sets were suitably equipped for this type of cab signaling from the start.

The trials continued with the first set though the autumn of 1959, but within a very short space of time, a number of difficulties appeared, which were highlighted as early as 27th November 1959 by AE Robson, the Chief Mechanical Engineer of the LMR at Euston. In a report

Facing page: Another Sam Lambert publicity view of an LMR set, with power car M60090 leading. The location is again Gorsey Bank crossing on the former Midland Railway Wirksworth branch. Of particular interest is the additional small window in the second of the twin doors giving access to the Guard's/luggage compartment. This is a plain door on other power cars, and it has not been possible to ascertain which vehicles were so fitted, or indeed why.

A first-class seat from one of the WR sets (also shown occupied within the colour section). Adjustment was possible between an upright or reclining seating position, although in the latter case, there could be a risk of collision with the person behind should they adopt a similar pose. Tabletops, regardless of class, were of Lanide material in French grey. One criticism of the internal layout referred to the difficulty that a tall passenger might have while entering or exiting a window seat, due to the longitudinal luggage rack. In contemporary publicity the comparison was made to airline travel, with the point being made that this rack was similar to those on an airliner (although, of course, no door lockers were provided). At that time, the majority of coaching stock on BR was still of the compartment type.

on that date, he commented on no less than 21 mechanical and other problems that would have to be rectified before the BR Commissioning Engineer would be satisfied that the trains could enter service. These included:

- Poor riding of the driving motor coaches, in which "the public could not be expected to sit".
- Intermittent loss of power from the Rolls-Royce auxiliary engines. This is not commented upon subsequently, and can be assumed to have been resolved satisfactorily.
- Oil leaks from the Brown-Boveri gear-cases, which were reported to be still noisy after 1,550 miles. The manufacturers commented that the noise would disappear after the mechanics had fully bedded-in, and that this should occur after 4,500 miles. There was no further comment on the oil leaks.
- Severe overheating of brake blocks causing distortion and cracking, attributed to the brake-block keys working loose on the motor and kitchen cars, when braking from above 40mph. The eventual cure was twofold; firstly, there was a change to a thicker type of brake block throughout, and secondly, the air-brake pressure was varied according to the vehicle and direction of travel. No doubt these changes in-

volved considerable trial and error, but they eventually came down to reducing the pressure from 65psi to 55psi on the leading power bogies, while on the non-powered bogies the pressure was increased to 80psi. Not clear from the paperwork is whether a similar 80psi was applied to the rear-most power bogies when they were trailing, and a similar question hangs over the effect that these changes might have made to the overall braking distances. Presumably, there must have been further high speed braking tests.

- Overheating of gas supply pipes in the kitchens, and ventilation problems in the kitchen cars, causing some burners to be extinguished at speeds above 60mph. Both of these were, presumably, cured.
- Overheating of floor-level heating grills in the passenger saloons, causing discomfort and the risk of setting fire to the fabric of the coach. There is no doubt that these matters were resolved, but again, no subsequent details are given.
- Ingress of rainwater through the kitchen doors, and of soot through the door ventilation grills when passing through tunnels. This was resolved, but what modifications were required to address this (and the

The front cover from the official Metropolitan-Cammell booklet that introduced the new trains, one page of which is also reproduced in colour elsewhere. Within its pages, care was taken to explain aspects of the design which were totally new to the public, and which included the question, "What is air-conditioning?" It was hoped that this facility would obviate the need to segregate smoking and non-smoking areas, and a note in official paperwork in 1961 refers to there being, "too much space devoted to non-smoking accommodation".

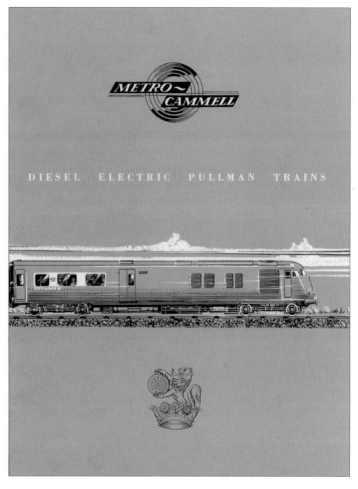

next three items) is not reported.

- Floor-level draughts throughout the train, and excessive draughts through the door seals in the entrance vestibules at speeds of more than 40mph.
- Problems with the continuity of the hot-water supply in the toilets. Tests showed that the warm water in toilets took 8 minutes to be replenished after use.
- Toilet vents too large, leading to toilet cubicles being cold.
- The pressure required to operate the passenger communication equipment varied between 26 and 36psi from vehicle to vehicle. It is not certain whether any changes were made, but there is an inordinate amount of surviving paperwork relating to the actual pressure required at each of the emergency communication cord points. Again, no final conclusions are to hand, but it might be that some changes took place subsequently, as a result of the variations to the brake pressure adjustments.
- Engine compartment temperature of 180°F, despite there being vents in floor and roof. This is perhaps one of the more interesting comments, as a note in the files refers to a circulating fan being fitted to the second train. The inference is that the now familiar roof fan fitted on all above-floor mounted railway engines was not initially thought necessary, and was a new innovation at this time.

- Flashover on No 4 traction motor. This was both an unfortunate and expensive failure, and as is usual with this type of defect was caused by a breakdown in the insulation. The only cure was a partial or complete strip-down and rewind of the commutator, depending on the degree of burning that had occurred.

Given the amount of trial and error associated with these trials, it is interesting to observe that it was not until some while after 1962 that the use of mathematical models was developed at BR's Derby research laboratories to study and predict the behaviour of wheels and running gear at speed.

It is well known that riding problems were the main concern, the report commenting that, "traction motors had never been fitted to the design of bogie beforehand". Even so, no cure was mentioned at this stage, and it again appears that trial and error prevailed rather than a considered engineering solution. Modifications included different strength springs; longer, 24-inch, swing-links mounted on rocking washers; and the installation of transverse hydraulic dampers (shock-absorbers). It was in this form, with the symptoms having been treated rather than the cause, that the trains entered service. It is believed that some of these modifications were applied first to the WR sets then on trial, and when found to be

Above: The interior of a WR second-class saloon, and again BR staff have been used, one of whom on the extreme right can be identified as Roy Morris from Paddington Public Relations Office (he later transferred to the SR). (It is easy to identify second class even in black and white photographs, as only a single Venetian blind was provided, with a single handle above the window for adjustment.) Straight-backed, non-adjusting seats were provided, which allowed for increased accommodation. There were some complaints from passengers (referred to within these pages) over the limited room available, particularly in second class, and while this might well have been true, JF Harrison, the CME of BR, drew the perfect comparison when he referred to the limited space available on an aircraft, "which is accepted without comment". Off the topic but relevant, is the fact that there is rarely a furore over air travel delays such as there is with train delays. The problem is heightened by the fact that other countries can seemingly run their railways exactly to schedule.

Opposite page: Further publicity views of passenger services, said to be aboard the LMR sets, although they would appear to be populated by the same people as on the WR trains! (Incidentally, first-class interiors can be identified by the blind controls at shoulder level, and by the corresponding vertical line in the centre of the window.) These views might have been taken around the time of the Press launch on 23rd June 1960, but regrettably, others from that date have not been located. Of the staff depicted, the senior man, wearing the shoulder braid, was Chris Lade, a long-serving Pullman employee, who hailed from Brighton, and was renowned for swimming in the sea every day. Chris was one of three men seconded from his usual Brighton Belle duties, first to the LMR, and then to the WR, with the intention of showing new starters the standard of Pullman service that was required. A number of Pullman stewards were ex-naval personnel, who were used to a strictly disciplined regime, as well as being courteous and efficient. The success of the trains was the cause of disputes between passengers on a number of occasions. More than half of all passengers would use the service on at least two occasions a week, and it therefore became exactly what had been intended, a form of travelling club. However, this caused difficulties with the oft-quoted phrase from Modern Railways, "How dare you sit in MY seat?" - the difficulty being that regular travellers would expect seats to be reserved for them without actually having booked them. This was particularly the case on the LMR working, although apparently the same applied on the Brighton Belle service as well. Around this time, various films were made, including the award winning 25-minute British Transport Films documentary from 1960, "Blue Pullman".

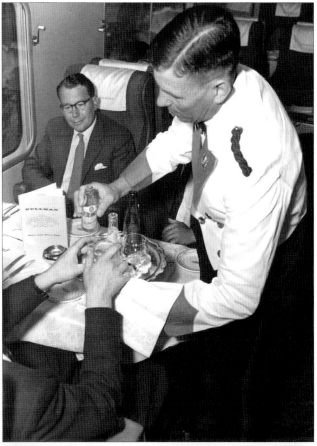

PULLMAN

Menu and Wine List

Scotch Smoked Salmon with Lemon wedges 7/6
Chilled Fruit Juices: Pineapple 1/6; Tomato 1/6; Orange 1/6
Crème Argenteuil with Golden Croutons 1/6

From the Grill

*English lamb Cutlets 8/6   *Scotch Salmon 8/6
* Fillet Steak 12/6   *Barbecued Chicken à l'Américaine 8/6

* Price of main dishes includes :

* Parsley, New and Olivette Potatoes, Sweet Corn, Baby Carrots
and Broccoli Mornay

Cold Buffet: Salmon Mayonnaise or
Half a Chicken with dressed Salads 8/6

Fresh Fruit Salad with dairy Cream Ice or
Crème Chantilly 2/-

Continental and English Cheese Tray 2/-

Coffee 8d

Bread Basket of White and Hovis Rolls
Ryvita and Curled Butter 6d

Menu and wine list from the WR operation in 1960. As a comparison, the first breakfast menu from the LMR service included scotch porridge and cream; cornflakes, puffed rice or frosted flakes; grapefruit cocktail; grapefruit juice, tomato juice or orange juice; poached haddock Colbert or grilled Royal kippers; omelette to your choice; bacon, egg and mushrooms; Oxford marmalade (orange or ginger) or honey; toast or oven rolls, and tea or coffee. The price was 7s 6d (37½p). A similarly extensive menu was available for afternoon tea, and later for dinner, which included such delights as melon, scampi, cold roast chicken, Yorkshire ham, roast beef, ox tongue, new potatoes, savarin printanaiere and Kirsch ice cream. A 1963 article in Modern Railways referred to the scope for individuality available to the Pullman Chef, with "some items available direct from Pullman stores, but with the chef also free use discretion as to whether to use the provided supplies or to cook for himself. Each chef on the train may order independently, but they can also draw on the others supplies if required. Food once cooked was rarely wasted as anything not served was used for staff meals." The implication is that the two chefs on each train could, in theory, be serving different menus, but this was not thought to be the case. It is not clear whether the same autonomy applied on the WR.

(Antony M Ford/David Hyde Collections)

successful the work was similarly undertaken on the Midland line trains. More detailed testing was destined to take place in 1961, and this is dealt with in Chapter 5.

With hindsight, it is surely nothing short of incredible that the sets were introduced to the Press and the public, in the knowledge that the riding was not up to the standard expected for a prestige luxury train. It is not right, even after all these years, to apportion blame to any particular organisation or individual, and it should be remembered that the pressures of modern business applied to all involved, the manufacturers, BR and the Pullman Car Co, as well as the engineers involved in the testing. So despite the trains' known shortcomings, there was a huge desire to see the sets enter revenue-earning service.

It is unlikely that anyone involved considered the situation to be in any way dangerous – just that the ride was less than satisfactory. The difference can be likened to paying for a Rolls-Royce, but finding comfort levels more akin to a modern sports car with hardened suspension.

It was originally intended to letter each car A to F (or A to H for the WR sets), but as each train would be maintained as two half-sets, it was realised that a set could be formed from two half-sets lettered A to C or A to D (and indeed, two half-sets lettered D to F or E to H). The resulting A-B-C-(D)-(D)-C-B-A formation would cause confusion over seat reservations, so removable plates were made up for each letter, which could be slipped into holders on the side of each car. In this way, the A to F or A to H lettering could be maintained, however the half-sets were marshalled together.

With each completed train set originally built to the same specification, the mechanical lessons learned from the trials of the first 6-car set would have to be applied to the remaining trains before they entered service, and it is believed the all the modifications were subsequently carried out at Derby, and in the case of the later WR sets, Swindon.

The start of 1960 saw both 6-car sets still either on trial or undergoing modification, but there was definite progress when, on 1st February, a complete train visited Manchester for the first time. This followed an exhilarating run north, which involved passing Bedford at 80mph and reaching a top speed of 105mph later on the journey.

Later that month, the first of the WR trains was involved in a distance test working as far as Mangotsfield, several runs being made to this destination via Barnt Green and Gloucester, and returning by the same route. The second WR train was delivered to Swindon at the end of March, but it was also noted that various modifications were still being carried out.

There is even a suggestion that the WR intended to usurp the LMR by being the first region to introduce the new trains into revenue-earning service, although a Paddington memorandum refers to the intended 1hr 50min Paddington to Birmingham timing having to be postponed indefinitely in April 1960 due to some signalling work not being completed. Exactly what this work was is unfortu-

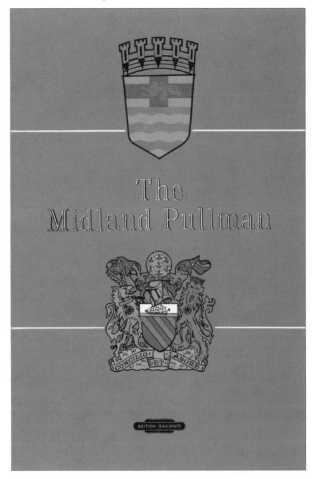

Publicity material for the Midland Pullman from 1960. This comprised a 12-page booklet incorporating photographs in colour and black and white, and line drawings that described both the new trains and also gave a brief resumé of the Pullman tradition. Of interest is the fact that the new train was also the first Pullman train on the LMS or BR(LMR) since 1933.

(Neville Bridger Collection)

nately not recorded.

In the meantime, the matters of staffing, staff training, infrastructure and maintenance also had to be dealt with, none of which attracted much attention in official documents at the time. Regardless of any difficulties that might have ensued, BR and Metropolitan-Cammell's pride in their achievement was demonstrated by a number of publicity films made at the time, almost exclusively in colour. As these films were made over time, it is clear that they involved more than one train, and differences in seating colours are apparent. Even so, they contribute an extremely valuable pictorial record of the period.

Notwithstanding the shortcomings in the trains' riding characteristics, BR was satisfied enough to approve the introduction of the trains into service on the ex-Midland Railway "Peak Route" between St Pancras and Manchester Central on and from 4th July 1960. No date for the announcement is known, but official approval for the trains to enter service was given by the British Rail-

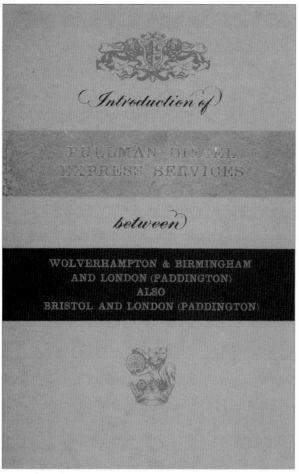

One of at least two brochures produced by the WR to launch their new service, and slightly more elaborate than the LMR version. This time, the booklet ran to 20 sides, and covered far more in the way of technical details, as well as a single page "Through the Window" type description for both the Bristol and Wolverhampton routes (in each direction, as well!) Illustrations were limited to a four-side colour centre section and a fold-out colour map inside the rear cover.

(David Hyde Collection)

ways Board on 4th June 1960.

A lavish Press launch was arranged for 23rd June 1960, Marylebone being chosen as the venue as it was close to the BRB Headquarters at 222 Marylebone Road (unkindly referred to in some quarters as "The Kremlin"). Marylebone had a long history as a location where new products were unveiled, in both LNER and BR days.

As a precursor to the Press launch, a complete train made probably its first visit to Marylebone on 29th May, with what would later become LMR Set 2, consisting of vehicles M60092, M60732, M60742, M60743 and M60093 (absent from the rake was TKFL, M60733, but it is not known why). After photographs and inspections, the set departed, possibly for High Wycombe. (Other contemporary reports refer to M60733 being present, but not M60092. This seems highly unlikely though, as

M60092 was a motor brake first and therefore formed one end of the train.)

On 23rd June 1960, both the 6- and 8-car sets were formally introduced to the Press, after which a special run was made, again to High Wycombe, carrying "the great and the good" in addition to journalists from Britain and overseas. Clearly the inclusion of Ambassadors and High Commissioners from a number of the, then, Commonwealth countries was with the intention of generating foreign orders, although in the event, none materialized. BR made every effort to ensure that the day passed without incident, with a veritable tome of paper orders distributed to ensure that the inspections, seating and trips passed off with military precision. The only difficulty encountered was with the windscreen wipers, which were reported as being continually blown back over the cab roof. This had already been noted during the trials, and was simply due to the effect of the slipstream at speed, accentuated no doubt by passing other trains, cuttings, bridges, and so on. It was later quickly and effectively remedied.

According to *British Railways Illustrated*, "one of the foremost railway commentators of the period, G Freeman Allen, was on the first press trip to High Wycombe and back, during which the Western unit attained 90mph". By inference, only the 8-car set was used for the trial run but this cannot be absolutely confirmed. The article went on, "Allen had been on the German TEE only the day before ('the most relaxing rail ride in Europe') but thought the Pullman rode noticeably harder over rail joints than the German trains, resulting in rattling crockery and 'visual evidence of vibration in the empty seats'. Allen took the view that this was a reflection of better welded track in Germany compared with the neglected old GC stuff out of Marylebone."

If the state of the track on the old Great Central was known to BR engineers (as it most certainly would have been) one wonders why Marylebone to High Wycombe was selected in the first place. It was possibly because this was simply the only route out of London with spare capacity at the time, although this could be challenged given that the runs took place outside peak hours. It is also suggested (in the *Railway Observer*) that a further Press trip was made the following day, 24th June, from Marylebone to High Wycombe.

A further Press run, this time for the benefit of the Manchester community, was made on 1st July 1960 (again, a prelude had taken place with a visit to Manchester on 30th June). The service was signalled away by the Lord Mayor of Manchester, and included in its compliment of VIP passengers, Sir John Elliot (Chairman of the Pullman Car Co), and Sir Reginald Wilson (Chairman of the LMR Board). On arrival at St Pancras, the train was quickly made ready for a round trip to Leicester to convey a number of businessmen, who were treated to luncheon *en-route*. An illustration of the front of the new trains appeared in *Design* for August 1960, and further publicity was obtained with another Press run sometime in November 1960, this time in the presence of news cameras from

DIESEL ELECTRIC PULLMAN TRAINS

Demonstration Run

FRIDAY, 24th JUNE 1960

VISIT OF
HIS EXCELLENCY
THE MINISTER OF COMMUNICATIONS, EGYPTIAN REGION
of the
UNITED ARAB REPUBLIC

LUNCHEON
on the
MIDLAND PULLMAN

FRIDAY. 12th AUGUST 1960

Further publicity material from the collection of Antony Ford. This time the covers of similar, but not identical, leaflets. The originals are approximately 7in x 4½in and printed with either light blue or dark blue lettering. Clearly it was not only BR who were trying to woo the customers, and Metropolitan-Cammell were looking towards the export market, although regrettably no orders would ever materialise. (Whether any even came close is not known.) The menus available on these occasions were of the set type, and did not offer the range of choices that would be available to the fare-paying passenger. "The Railway Gazette" reported no less than 84 from the ranks of "the great and the good ... and hopefully the influential as well", who were allotted seats on the occasion of 24th June, although these were only the invited and it cannot be certain how many actually travelled.

Around the same time, a number of newspaper articles and features appeared including coverage in "The Times", "The Daily Telegraph", "The Star", and at least one of the London evening newspapers. The article in "The Times" took the form of a full page advertisement, complete with 11 illustrations covering the journey and what could be achieved: "The pointer for the businessman with an important job to do in another place – and who wants to count the time between well spent ... luxury for the man who works hard and lives well." There followed a series of timed events: "8.45 – Morning Departure. Five minutes before leaving, he's greeted by a friendly attendant. Just one of the crew who will see to his slightest wish on the smooth, fast, comfortable journey from Manchester to London. 8.47 – Luggage for the 'in' tray. Metal racks for bags, attendant to stack the racks, enclosed compartments for heavy luggage. 10.15 – Shift to neutral. Work finished, armchair reclined: a foam-rubber and air conditioned atmosphere for relaxation. 12.30 – London just down the steps, reached at the right time for the West End or City luncheon date – and the afternoon for conferences. 5.30 – Business over. Off for last appointment: the train back. 6.10 – Evening departure. VIP greeted at the door, seen to seat, settled in. And activity starts at the bar, the pick-me-up service for the man in a feet-up mood at the end of the London trip. 7.30 – Table for four travellers. Dinner at leisure during transportation at top speed. Behind the scenes: kitchens gleaming like a chef's day-dream; wine at fine as a gourmet's. 9.5 – End of the evening, after a meal to match the elegance and good taste of the surroundings. Brandy, cigar, a light at hand; Manchester 15 minutes off. Business – and pleasure – complete."

the BBC, ITV and cinema newsreels. It is not clear if this involved the LMR or WR set, but it is possible that one of the spare sets was used.

The public introduction of the new trains, particularly on the LMR, was also carefully stage-managed, considerable care being taken to ensure that staff were briefed, pantries were stocked and advice given as to the suggested wording to be used by staff when making public announcements. Indeed, a list of announcements was prepared and issued to staff, although it was stated that is was to be considered only as a guide. One of the suggestions, relating to the departure of the up service from Manchester in the morning was, "Good morning ladies and gentlemen, welcome to the Blue Pullman. In a few minutes we shall stop at Cheadle Heath to take on more passengers, after which breakfast will be served

On the LMR, two trains were available, but only one was used, the other being retained as a stand-by. This was costly exercise, but was one that was very much appreciated by the public, whose initial response was almost immediate and universal acclamation. The result was that even with the supplementary fare that was charged, business travellers flocked to the service, and loadings were often 100% in the all-first class train.

On the WR, a mixture of first and second class accommodation was available, the service commencing on 12th September 1960 with a morning train from Bristol Temple Meads to Paddington, and another from Wolverhampton calling at Birmingham Snow Hill, also terminating at Paddington. Return runs to both destinations occurred in the evening. The WR therefore required regular use of two of its sets, the third acting as spare.

Ironically, despite the innovation in technology represented by the new units, one throwback to Victorian times still remained, as the Midland (to start with, at least) continued the tradition of using an old-fashioned, oil tail-lamp at the rear. The WR however grasped the new technology and used the centre marker light on the trailing power car fitted with a red shade.

None of this would have been possible without an agreement, hammered out in the early months of 1960, between BR and the National Union of Railwaymen (NUR) stating that existing BR restaurant car staff would be seconded to the Pullman Car Co. BR also gave an undertaking that no further expansion of Pullman services would take place unless, and until, a long-term agreement had been reached over the wider question of rail catering on both conventional and Pullman services.

1960 witnessed the introduction of the new trains, and also the peak of their success. The Blue Pullmans were referred to as "Midland Pullman" on the LMR, but understandably just "Pullman" by the WR, and these designations were carried above the windows on each. Unfortunately, the honeymoon would not last long, as economic pressures required maximum stock utilization, while the trains were plagued by consistent complaints about their rough riding. The peak years for the trains commenced in 1960, but would be short-lived - indeed it

could even be argued that it was downhill all the way from 1960.

HOW TO IGNORE IT
(without breaking the law)

TRAVEL MIDLAND PULLMAN
it touches 90 mph

A slightly later, and perhaps more subtle, approach to publicity. A similar design was used for contemporary newspaper advertising.

(Antony M Ford Collection)

Blasting away from Paddington, a WR set leaves a trail of diesel fumes on a test run – ostensibly on 5ᵗʰ September 1959. The date is taken from the rear of what was noted as a BR(WR) official photograph, although its accuracy must be called into question as records from the National Archive at Kew refer to the first of the WR sets having only been delivered in November 1960.

On 16ᵗʰ June 1960, a demonstration run was undertaken by the WR for Brigadier Langley, Chief Inspecting Officer at the Ministry of Transport (WR Report W124). This was considered necessary as this was the first time the existing WR AWS (the original GWR term ATC was not used in the report) had been used with an air-brake system as fitted to the new trains. A note in the report stated that, "For the inspection of the equipment, it will be necessary to see it both in the laboratory and on the multiple unit stock, opened out for view as much as possible. The test should be on a high-speed stretch of track, and it should include both movement at very slow speed over ramps and braking tests under high- and medium-speed AWS conditions with the regulator (a "steam" term) in the power position if applicable." The section of line chosen for the test was between Swindon and Stoke Gifford (the Badminton Line).

The trial took place in both directions, and an 8-car formation with power cars W60098 and W60099 was used. At the time, the brake pressure on the WR sets was limited to 50psi at all times on the power cars, and also on the motor bogies of the auxiliary power cars; a maximum of 70psi applied to all the other vehicles. These figures were in accordance with the latest decision of the CME of BR. In the down direction, the tests were carried out on the ruling 1 in 300 falling gradients at Brinkworth, Coalpit Heath and Winterbourne, while for the return run, tests were carried out at Winterbourne, Chipping Sodbury and Brinkworth. In all cases, the distant signals displayed a caution aspect. The results of the tests, with speeds varying between 59.8mph and 89.6mph, showed stopping distances between 665yd and 1,521yd, although even in the latter case, at the highest speed, this was still 433yd in rear of the home signal.

On one occasion it was noted that, despite striking the ramp at caution, the speed continued to rise for a further three seconds because the train was accelerating at the time. This was not considered to be a problem as the required stopping distances had been achieved. It would appear from the report that during the tests, some variations were made to the pressure applied to the bogies with as little as 50psi to the power cars, 55 to 50psi to the motor bogie of the auxiliary power cars, 70 to 50psi to the trailing bogie of the same vehicle, and 70 to 50psi to the parlour cars. Any subsequent modifications or conclusions are not reported, although it appears that the Inspecting Officer was satisfied with the performance, as services started a few weeks later.

Power Car M60093 in posed mode, probably forming part of LMR set 2. The finding of this, and several of the other ac-companying views in this section, was particularly fortuitous, bearing in mind the present inaccessibility of the main Metropolitan-Cammell archive. A conversation with Pete Waterman from Just Like the Real Thing revealed that he had located a series of photographs that had once been in the hands of Rosebud and were used by their design team to assist in the production of the "OO" scale Kitmaster models in the 1960s. Such items might be expected to have long-since vanished, but their survival enables a number of detail views to be included, and will no doubt assist a new generation of modellers over 40 years later. (*Pete Waterman/Just Like the Real Thing Collection*)

Chapter 4

A MECHANICAL AND AESTHETIC INTERLUDE

A mechanical description of what was officially referred to as the "British Railways Diesel-Electric Pullman Trains" was given in an extensive article in *The Railway Gazette* on 24th June 1960. Much of what follows is taken (with due acknowledgement) from that source, and is supplemented by additional items as indicated. Other descriptions, limited in some detail, have appeared elsewhere, but the one from *The Railway Gazette* ranks highly amongst the engineering fraternity, and because it is contemporary, was no doubt sourced from the manufacturers themselves. It has been included here in full, and comments and deviations from the original text are included in italics and in brackets. From a number of points included in the descriptions that follow, it would appear to relate more to the LMR sets. There is also a reference to the ladies' toilet within the description, as was mentioned on page 12.

Following an extensive period of service trials, British Railways will shortly introduce the first of a batch of de-luxe diesel-electric Pullman trains designed for high-speed travel, with superior standards of comfort and a personal service of meals and refreshments for all travellers. These trains, which have been supplied to British Railways by the Metropolitan-Cammell Carriage & Wagon Co Ltd, are powered by two 1,000bhp NBL/MAN diesel engines, each direct-coupled to a GEC main generator. The complete order is for five trains, two of which are six-car trains for first-class passengers only, and three are of eight cars with first and second class accommodation. The six-car train will run in the London Midland Region, on the main line between Manchester Central, London St Pancras and Leicester, and the eight-car trains in the Western Region between Bristol, London Paddington, and Wolverhampton, Birmingham and Paddington.

Passenger accommodation is in enclosed saloons,

M60093 complete in blue livery with red buffer stocks. Although brand new at this stage, clearly testing has resulted in the accumulation of dirt on the bogies and a minor dent has also been acquired. The first pair of shutter grills on the engine compartment appear to be open.
(Pete Waterman/Just Like the Real Thing Collection)

Pre-service trials of M60093 and LMR Set 2. Notice on the second vehicle, an MKFL (Motor-Kitchen-First-Lavatory), the lack of uniformity over the continuation of the white livery. This would date the view as probably pre-February 1960, but certainly before the entry to public service (see page 17). As with several views around this time, the park position of the wipers has yet to be resolved.

(Pete Waterman/Just Like the Real Thing Collection)

and all seats on the de-luxe trains are reserved. The Driver and Guard are linked by Loudaphone, and a public address system is installed throughout the train. Under-floor-mounted diesel-driven generating sets supply power for lighting and auxiliary services. *(This was an interesting concept and meant that the output of the engines need not be sacrificed for auxiliary needs. As a comparison, the later HST sets, albeit with a considerably higher combined power output of 4,400bhp, could see a reduction in available power of 10-20%, depending on the demands made according to external climatic conditions, for example. The underfloor engines have, in the past, given rise to the incorrect assertion that they constituted an auxiliary "power car". However, these engines were provided solely for the purpose of supplying auxiliary power, and could not be used to supplement the output available from the engines mounted in the power cars. This confusion has been heightened as the powered bogies driving the train forward, regardless of six or eight car type, were always the rear bogie of the power car and the leading bogie of the second vehicle.)*

The livery is Nanking Blue *(this was the official name for the colour, although it also had the alternative name, Cambridge Blue)*, relieved by a broad white band

extending the length and width of the windowed section along the sides of each car. The rounded nose of each motorcar features the Pullman Car Co Ltd crest, and this is also carried on the white-painted band between the last pair of windows on each vehicle. *(The crest, or more accurately, coat of arms, was applied by transfer. Its presence was suggested by Arthur Wolstenholme, and was to a design that was an elongation of the conventional Pullman crest. The revised design was the work of Milner Gray of the Design Research Unit. The same modified crest was also used later on the 1960s Pullman vehicles for the Eastern Region.)* The roofs are painted light grey, the underframes aluminium, and the bogies black.

Principal dimensions and data are as follows:

Maximum service speed	90mph
Weight of train – 6 car	299 tons
Weight of train – 8 car	364 tons
Fuel capacity	1,000 gallons

(Fuel was carried in four tanks of equal capacity, and was considered sufficient for 900 miles in normal service. Interestingly, the LMR quoted that the fuel capacity would be sufficient to cover 1,000 miles, so presumably the dif-

Rear view of a power car, showing the buffing gear and Stone-Kheop electrical connections. Two works plates will be noted; the wording is "BR Metro Cammell Lot No 30554 1959", making this particular vehicle a DMBS for the WR (see Appendix A).

(Pete Waterman/Just Like the Real Thing Collection)

The main engine compartment, viewed from the doorway into the cab. The two button panel is for local engine control, start-stop. To the right is the "Push to check lub oil level" button.

Main and auxiliary generators of the power car; the unit above the generator housed the servo-regulator. The fire Claxton can be seen on the right-hand ceiling.

ference was due to the variation in weight between a 6- and 8-car train.)

Length of vehicles over body: Motor Car: 66ft 5½in
                               Trailer Car: 65ft 6in

Overall height	12ft 4½in
Overall width	9ft 6in
Bogie centres	46ft
Bogie wheelbase	9ft 6in

The six-car trains are made up of two power cars, two combined kitchen and passenger cars, and two parlour cars. In the power car, the cooling group, with side radiators and roof-mounted fan, is immediately behind the driving cab bulkhead. A bulkhead across the generator, with doors at each side, divides the engine and generator compartments. Separate cubicles are used for housing the HT and LT equipment. *(Access to the engine for maintenance was by three roller shutters, one larger than the other two, on each side of the power car.)* Adjoining the generator compartment is the Guard and luggage compartment, the partitions of which are sound insulated. This compartment has access doors to the passenger saloon and to the power compartment. *(A periscope was provided for the Guard, and double doors of standard BR design gave access to the van and the limited luggage area.)*

The saloon accommodates 12 passengers *(18 in the WR power cars, which were all second class)*; at the gangway end is a ladies' toilet on one side and a small luggage compartment on the other. *(In the Midland sets, the passenger compartment within the power car was 15ft long. In the WR trains it was 20ft long. The window spacing on the Midland power cars also made them immediately distinguishable from their sister units operating out of Paddington, with the former having two large and one small window on each side. The WR sets had three windows of equal size and spacing.)*

Opposite page, top: Seconded SR Pullman Inspector Cullen (left), an unknown member of staff and Conductor Lade (right) await the passengers. *(Pete Waterman/Just Like the Real Thing Collection)*
Opposite page, bottom: The powered bogie at the rear of M60092. (Pete Waterman/Just Like the Real Thing Collection)

The gangway into a first-class parlour car (Type 6) with the swing door into the seating area open. Luggage space was available alongside what was originally intended to be the Gents lavatory at this end of the vehicle. (A Ladies lavatory was originally so designated at the opposite end.) The similarity of the internal layout with later designed Mark 3 rolling stock is apparent. Facing, on the right with the grille above was a control panel at what was deemed the "lobby" end of the coach. This control panel, accessed with a standard BR1 key, controlled the individual air conditioning for that particular vehicle. Running numbers for vehicles of this type were 60740 — 60749. Plan layouts of this and the other types of car are shown on pages 19 through 21.

The passenger accommodation in the kitchen car is an 18-seat non-smoking saloon. At the gangway end is a toilet, and luggage and equipment cupboards. Adjacent to the saloon is the pantry, and at the gangway end of the kitchen is the staff accommodation. In the parlour car, 36 seats are provided, with a toilet and a luggage compartment at each end. In the six-car train, the total seating is 132 first-class.

The eight-car train has additional seating in the power cars and two additional parlour cars for second-class passengers. The total seating capacity is 228, 108 of which are first class and 120 second class.

The entrance vestibules at the ends of the cars are wide and spacious, and the access gangways between the cars are also wider than normal width. The gangways are mounted on pivots at the ends of each vehicle. When joined together, these semi-floating units between pairs of cars form a level platform free from the normal gangway oscillation. Rubber seals cover the outside of the gangways and prevent draughts and loss of air-conditioned air. *(The gangways were of the Swiss-type, Metro SIG, and were similar to those on the Swiss Federal Railways lightweight stock. A non-slip rubber floor plate was also provided.)*

The complete train is fully air-conditioned with automatic control of air temperature and humidity. The inward flow of air to the saloons from the air-conditioning plant is through outlets in a duct concealed by the central lighting panel. Fully adjustable Venetian blinds are fitted between the glasses of the double-glazed windows. Particular care has been taken to achieve a high standard of sound insulation, and track noise has been reduced to a

Interior of a first-class WR set. Passengers could summon an attendant with a button located near to the table lamp (visible in several of the interior views). This would illuminate a green light, visible above the centre line of the adjacent window; the cancel button can be seen at the top of the table leg. With typical British reserve, most passengers would wait until an attendant was passing rather than use the call facility.

(Antony M Ford Collection)

low level. The insulated floors are fully suspended.

In each car, the seating is arranged in facing pairs on one side of the passenger gangway, and in facing individual seats on the other, with double or single fixed tables respectively set between them. All seating is of the armchair type, with deep foam-rubber cushions upholstered in red- or blue-striped fabric trimmed with black and grey plastic hide. *(According to George Behrend writing in his book* Pullman in Europe *in 1962, "The first class saloons are finished off in two colour schemes. In one, the seats are furnished in red upholstery with navy blue stripes, with a blue and black carpet and rosewood partitions at the ends. In the other, light blue with navy blue stripes is used for the upholstery, and the carpet is red and black, while the partitions are ebony." Behrend also confirms the colour of the upholstery in the Western*

Region second-class cars as, "blue with black stripes and the carpet red and black". A second opinion from Charles Long, confirms that first class on both the LMR and WR sets were either red ribbed or blue ribbed, each half-set being of a different combination; a similar arrangement applied to the LMR power cars. Therefore, depending on whether or not identically upholstered half-sets were connected together, the first-class upholstery could either be half one colour and half the other or identical throughout. On the WR, second-class upholstery was always blue, but in a different shade to that used in first class.) The first-class seats can be adjusted from the reclining to the upright position, and are mounted on runners for fore and aft adjustment at the table. In the second-class saloon, the seats are of the same armchair type, but are not adjustable.

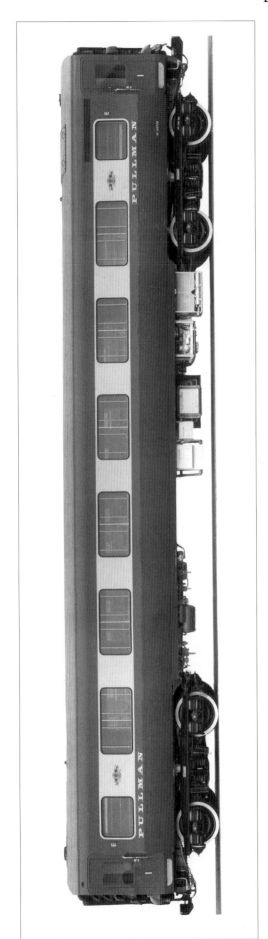
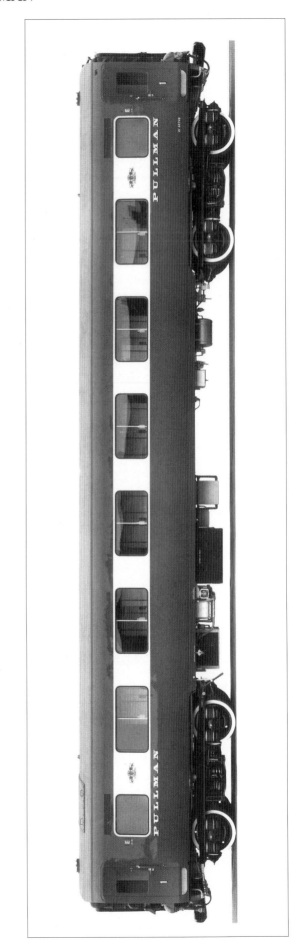

WR first-class parlour cars. None of the vehicles ever carried names, and indeed this was never intended to be the case. Possibly in view of Sir John Elliot's unmoving stance on the issue of table lamps, it might be expected that this would have been an issue as well. (The body and chassis of each vehicle was of integral construction, stress relieved and incorporated the judicious use of welding.)

(Pete Waterman/Just Like the Real Thing Collection)

The interior décor, which varies from vehicle to vehicle, has been chosen to give pleasing and colourful combinations, mainly of decorative rosewood and ebony veneers, grey plastic hide, plastic seating and contrasting seat upholstery. The partitions forming the ends of each passenger saloon are decorated with wood veneers and abstract plastic inlays. Each partition has glazed panels in the access door, the glass having a vertical striped pattern, ⅜in apart, which acts as a mirror, but allows unimpeded vision at close quarters. *(These mirrors were favourably received by passengers. In addition to the vehicles themselves, Jack Howe oversaw all the design details, such as the crockery and cutlery used on the trains.)*

The bodyside walls are faced with plastic hide from floor level up to the continuous hand-luggage racks running along the length of each passenger saloon. Above the racks, walls and ceiling surfaces are lined with plastic in pearl-grey, with a fine black-line pattern superimposed, which continues up to the central lighting panel in the ceiling.

The exposed parts of the hand-luggage racks, the table edges, and window surrounds are all of anodised aluminium, satin finished in aluminium for the first class, and in pale gold for the second class. The heater grilles, mounted low on the bodyside alongside the seats, are of satin-finished stainless steel.

Floor carpets, in kingfisher blue or cardinal red, *(again depending upon the corresponding upholstery seat colour)* are fitted on plastic underlay. The walls of the entrance vestibules at the car ends are faced in pearl-grey plastic, with plastic hide trimming around the inter-car gangway entrances. Coir mat floor covering is used in the vestibules.

In each saloon, the main lighting is by twin warm-white fluorescent tubes in the centre of the ceiling, supplemented by tungsten lamps fitted in the luggage racks above each table. The fluorescent tubes are placed end-to-end, and covered by flush-jointed diffusion panels. When illuminated, the tubes show as a continuous panel of light running the length of the saloon. Individual table lamps, with glass shades, are mounted on swan-necked pillars fixed to the bodyside just below window level. *(Considerable care had to be given in the placing of these auxiliary lamps, the politics behind which were discussed in a previous chapter. The fact that it would be necessary to change the tablecloths on a regular basis was probably the reason why the lamps were not attached directly to the tables.)* Battery operated emergency lighting is also installed.

The kitchen and pantry accommodation is well arranged for ease of working under the most hygienic conditions. The gas cooking range is fitted across one end, and the refrigerator adjacent to the pantry partition. Two of the four extractor fans are located above the cooker. Worktops are arranged on the corridor side, with the sinks, sterilizing units, and water boilers along the bodyside. All kitchen utensils, sink units, and working tops are in stainless steel. The walls are lined with pearl-grey plastic finish, and the ceilings matt white. The floors are of red composition material set in a two-inch square mesh aluminium grill. A staff compartment and lavatory are provided adjacent to the gangway entrance to the car. *(A single 200-gallon water tank supplied water for each kitchen car, and was also used for the staff toilet.)*

The equipment of the well-appointed toilets includes *(paper)* towel dispensers and hygienic spray washing facilities, which give an automatically timed flow of water. Water temperature of the timed flow can be regu-

Kitchen facilities. The sterilizer mentioned in the text is the open area nearest the camera with the sink beyond. Not clear from the photograph was the provision of a floor drain to cope with water spillage. At the far end can be seen the gas range with fume chamber over. The serving hatch opening onto the corridor area is also visible on the left.

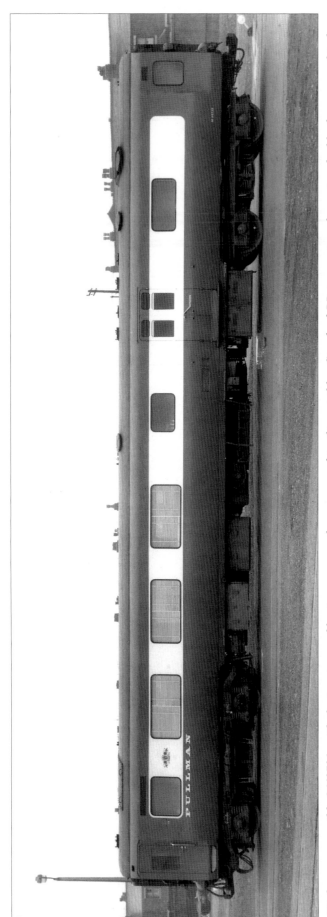

Kitchen car, possibly M60731, with the two types of bogie necessary for power and trailing visible. Standard BR-type outward-opening double doors were fitted on each side of the kitchen car, one set giving access to the passenger corridor. These enabled easy restocking of the vehicle from either side at the various termini. This design, which incorporated the auxiliary engine was designated type 4, the WR variant was type 5 but with a "heavy" bogie under the kitchen end. In both cases they were designated as non-smoking.

(Pete Waterman/Just Like the Real Thing Collection)

End view of a TKFL from Lot 30557 for the Western Region. The single builders plate will be noted. Although different to the LMR vehicles below the solebar, the passenger and kitchen accommodation was identical in both types. On the LMR vehicles the auxiliary engine provided power for a 400v 3-phase 50-cycle (Hertz) supply at a maximum of 190amp. 24-volt lead-acid batteries were also provided for emergency and stand-by services. The normal running speed for the auxiliary engines was 1,500rpm, with various coloured lights visible both internally and externally indicating normal, stand-by or fault conditions. In practice only one auxiliary unit was operated, and it was only if the exterior temperature was below 45°F that both would be needed. The air-conditioning system also pressurised the interior of the passenger compartments very slightly, so instructions were given to ensure that the exterior doors were only open for the minimum time.
(Pete Waterman/Just Like the Real Thing Collection)

lated as required. The walls are plastic faced in flame, clover pink, and grey, and the ceilings painted matt white. Coloured mosaic paving is used for the floor. Metal fittings are finished in satin chromium plate, with the exception of the skirting beadings of satin-finished anodised aluminium and the satin-finished stainless steel heater and ventilation grills. Separate toilet accommodation is provided for ladies. *(The water tank capacity for each lavatory was 70 gallons. A minor criticism of the toilet facilities was that the automatic washing facility cut the water off too quickly. However, praise was given for the florescent lighting built into the mirrors.)*

Power for the main auxiliary generators is supplied by the NBL/MAN, 12-cylinder, supercharged, diesel engine type L12V18/21BS having a 12-hr rating of 1,000bhp at 1,500rpm. Cylinder dimensions are 180mm bore and 210mm stroke. A considerable number of engines of this type are in use for diesel-electric and diesel-hydraulic traction. *(The D8xx, D61xx and D63xx diesel locomotives all used the same type of engine, but at power outputs varying between 1,000 and 1,100bhp. The Pullman engines were built as a V12 design.)*

Individual cylinder heads are of the pre-combustion type, provided with two inlet- and two ex-

Close up detail of the non-powered front bogie.

(Pete Waterman/Just Like the Real Thing Collection)

haust-valves. Supercharging is by a Napier, exhaust-gas, turbo blower mounted above the generator drive. At the free end of the engine is the crankshaft-driven pump for the hydraulic motor fan drive. CAV fuel injection equipment and an Ardleigh governor are fitted. Lubrication priming before starting is by a Mirlees pump driven by a GEC motor. A belt-driven Dowty pump feeds the fuel-service tank.

Warning lamps are fitted to indicate low water level, high water temperature, low oil pressure, overload, and earth fault, and the engine idling speed is automatically reduced to idling in the event of high water temperature, overload, or earth fault. In each driving cab is fitted a general warning light and a light to indicate when an engine has stopped.

The combined engine/generator unit is mounted on a common fabricated steel bedplate and installed on Metalastik anti-vibration mountings. The use of a quick-running Vee engine results in a good power-weight ratio.

The Serck cooling group, comprising vertical radiator panels in the bodyside and roof-mounted extractor fan, (*not to be confused with the fan later provided to limit the engine compartment temperature*) is positioned

behind the cab bulkhead in the power car. The cooling fan, which is 45in diameter, is driven at the correct speed to suit the cooling required by the Serck-Behr hydrostatic fan drive. The hydraulic fan motor is supplied with oil under pressure by the engine-driven pump, via a thermostatically controlled by-pass valve. Until the engine coolant reaches the minimum operating temperature, the pump delivery is by-passed to the oil tank: during this time the fan remains stationary. At normal operating temperatures the by-pass is closed and the resulting oil pressure rise causes the radiator shutters to open, and the fan to be driven at a speed corresponding to the amount of cooling required. Access from the cab to the power compartment is through the radiator tunnel.

The main generator is a self-ventilated, single-bearing machine with windings for separately excited, and self-excited main fields and a series decompounding winding. This also forms part of the series excitation for motorising the generator for engine starting. The continuous ratings at 1,500rpm are 1,700A 383 V or 1,250A 523V, 650kW.

The armature shaft also carries the armature of the auxiliary generator mounted at the rear end. The ventilat-

Power car underframe detail. The power cars had steel underframes, whereas the other vehicles were of integral construction. Each power car had a 250-gallon fuel tank, while each auxiliary engine had 100-gallon tank. Notice also the standard speedometer take-off. (Pete Waterman/Just Like the Real Thing Collection)

ing fan at the drive end draws cooling air through both machines. The auxiliary generator is rated at 91A 110V, 10kW, the voltage being held within close limits throughout the engine speed range by a Newton automatic voltage regulator. This generator supplies excitation for the main generator and current for starter-battery charging, control circuits, and other auxiliaries.

The main generator output is controlled by an automatic load regulator, which in turn is controlled by the engine speed governor. This method of control ensures that the full engine output available at each notch setting made by the driver is maintained over a wide range of train speeds. The power output of the generators at each end of the train is accurately synchronized. Protection against wheel-slip is provided by a current limiting relay.

The air-conditioning equipment is designed to provide and maintain an automatically controlled clean comfortable atmosphere within established limits of temperature and humidity irrespective of outside ambient conditions. This requires provision for heating, cooling, air filtration, car insulation and a degree of manual temperature selection for service requirements. In addition to the attraction of a high standard of passenger comfort, the air conditioning also keeps clean and fresh the upholstery, fittings, and other equipment. *(There was a belief at the time that air conditioning would eliminate the need to segregate smokers and non-smokers, but this did not work out in practice.)*

Each car is equipped with a roof-mounted air conditioning unit, floor heaters, automatic control panel, and a refrigeration unit. The conditioning unit filters the air, removes excess moisture, and either cools or heats the air as required. *(In this respect the phrase "climate-control unit" would perhaps have been more appropriate, but this would have been an unfamiliar term whereas "air-conditioning" was understood and was perceived to be the latest in comfort.)*

A proportion of the air in the car is extracted by roof ventilators, and this is made up by admitting filtered fresh air into the system. Heating is by electric heaters, and cooling is by flowing the air over the evaporator coils of the refrigerator. Excess moisture is deposited as dew on the cold coils of the evaporator.

The motor-driven compressor and condenser are mounted on the underframe, and use Freon 12 or Arcton 12 as a refrigerant. *(Both are CFC compounds and would not now be permitted. In 1960, of course, the risk such products presented to the atmosphere was not known.)* The condenser is cooled by motor-driven fans. The manual temperature control switch enables the heaters to be switched on at car temperatures of 68°F, 71°F or 74°F, automatic control being by Vapor thermostats. To ease the load on the power supply if the air-conditioning

This page: The control desk, as seen from the driver's side. Note that the crew seat folded forward and down, to enable easy entry through the cab door.

(Pete Waterman/Just Like the Real Thing Collection)

Opposite: Cab and controls. The interior was painted grey with a white ceiling. Later a notice was provided above the window which stated "Maximum speed under power or coasting 90mph". Adjustable seats were provided for both members of the crew, and although not visible in the photograph, there was also an electric stove for cooking, while noise was reduced by fibreglass insulation between the cab and the engine compartment. The LMR and WR cabs were basically identical, although there was the addition of ATC on the WR units (the equivalent AWS was not provided on the LMR trains until 1962). From the outset, there was a "deadman's treadle" under the control desk. An alarm bell was provided to warn of a fire in the engine compartment, and three separate fire extinguishers were provided. In the extreme left-hand corner can be seen the Loudaphone communication equipment use by the Driver and Guard. Train crews recall that the sets were bouncy to ride on, and have made comparisons to what were later designated the Class 25 diesels.

(Pete Waterman/Just Like the Real Thing Collection)

compressors throughout the train were switched on simultaneously, a delay switch is fitted to give a sequenced switching throughout the train.

Current for lighting, air conditioning, refrigeration, battery charging and auxiliary equipment is supplied by two underfloor generator sets, each set comprising an eight-cylinder, Rolls-Royce, horizontal diesel engine direct-coupled to a Stones Tonum alternator. The output of one set is sufficient for normal summer and winter requirements; the second set is carried for use as a stand-by, and for use under extreme conditions. The engine is rated at 190bhp at 1,500rpm, and the three-phase 50-cycle alternator at 133kVA, 400V.

In the six-car train, the generating sets are mounted underneath each of the kitchen cars and in the eight-car trains they are underneath the second-class parlour cars.

Provision is made for the operation of the lighting, refrigeration, and air-conditioning equipment from an external three-phase AC supply when the train is stationary.

Close up detail of the coupling between vehicles. A special form of jumper connection between the cars uses butt contacts to eliminate possible misalignment with the plug and socket type. The connections were used for both power and control circuit wiring.

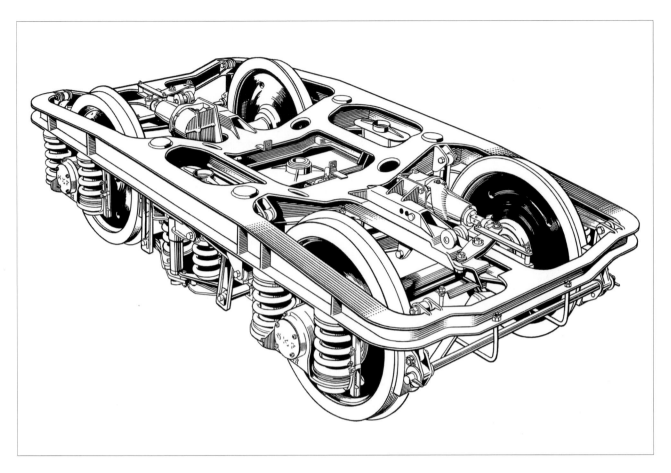

Taken from the Metropolitan-Cammell brochure (the cover of which can be seen on page 27) giving detail of the basic Metro-Schlieren carrying bogie. The frames of the leading and motor bogies were fabricated from special steel pressings although, in terms of damping, the principals displayed here and referred to in the text still applied.

Static power supply points are being provided at terminal stations on the routes to be served by these trains.

(At first sight, the LMR and WR sets appeared similar externally, other than the fact that the number of cars differed. However, as has been mentioned, there were several differences, such as window spacing in the power cars, seating, upholstery, and the location of the auxiliary generating equipment. Additionally, due to differences in the formation the second driving bogie was located under the kitchen first on the LMR trains and under the parlour second on the WR. This is discussed further in Appendix A. The requirement to accommodate second-class passengers on the WR sets also meant that the space dedicated per passenger was reduced and so the window spacing was altered on the second-class parlour cars to seven a side, compared with six for first class. This, at least, afforded each passenger a clear outward view, which was in direct contrast to the standard bodyshell used on later BR coaches where some passengers were faced with a blank wall.)

The 400V AC, three-phase, 50-cycle power for lighting and air-conditioning is distributed by two four-wire feeders running the length of the train. Connections between the cars are made through Stone Kleops intercar couplings, and the circuits so arranged that if a coupling is broken the feeder is immediately disconnected from the power-supply. The bulk of the lighting is supplied at 230V AC by phase-to-neutral connection of the 400V feeders, and the remainder is supplied at 110V AC from a 230/110V lighting transformer. The compressor, condenser-fan motor, and the floor and air heaters are connected to the three-phase, 400V supply. The air-conditioning fan motor and the control circuits are supplied at 24V DC from a three-phase transformer/rectifier unit. This supply is also used to charge a 24V, 216amp-hour battery for auxiliary engine starting and emergency lighting.

The bogies are of the Metro-Schlieren type *(this design, with modifications, was used for both the powered and non-powered bogies)*, incorporating hydraulically-damped helical springs. At each end of the train formation there are two traction motors in the inner bogie of the power car and two in the adjacent bogie of the vehicle coupled next to it, making eight axles motorised in a train of either six or eight coaches.

The unsprung weight on the axle is reduced to a minimum by carrying the motor on a three-point mounting on the bogie frame. To accommodate the relative ver-

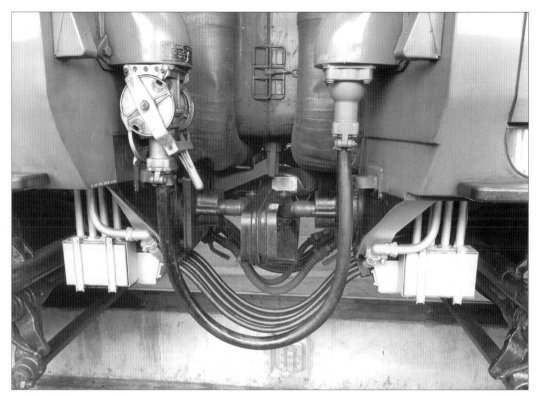

Coach coupling detail. The small notice reads "Danger. Coupling bolts must not be removed until tension between cars is taken up by auxiliary screw couplings." It is believed that screw couplings were not provided as a permanent feature between the vehicles and accordingly would need to be obtained from a maintenance depot.

tical movement of the axle and motor, the motor drive is taken through a Brown-Boveri spring drive unit. On the motor shaft is mounted a single helical reduction gear, meshing with the axle-drive gear which is mounted on a quill shaft carried on roller bearings. In the face of the gear is a ring of spring-loaded pads which engage with face-dogs integral with a spider pressed on the road wheel hub. Thus the gears are maintained at the correct centres while allowing free vertical movement between axle and motor.

The motors are four-pole, self-ventilated machines with a continuous rating of 425A 383V 199hp at 1,360rpm and a gear ratio of 19/67. The two motors in each power bogie are in parallel. Current for the inner-vehicle power-car motors is supplied through cables attached to the adjacent power car.

Special features are incorporated in the Westinghouse air-brake equipment to maintain the high efficiency at high speed. Control is by electro-pneumatic valves, and at train speeds at which normal braking is required, the degree of standard brake pressure applied to the cylinders is proportional to the position of the Driver's brake controller.

In the high-speed range, the brake pressure is automatically increased to compensate for the lower coefficient of friction of the cast-iron shoes when operating at high speed. The changeover from high-speed to normal-speed braking, and *vice-versa*, is entirely automatic, and is controlled by a valve energized by current from the speedometer generator. The de-luxe Pullmans are the first trains to be fitted with two stage EP braking. *(The Electro-pneumatic brake was universally used by the Southern Region on its multiple unit electric stock and was renowned for its efficiency.)*

Operating through switch contacts in the controller, the standard brake valve handle is also used to control the automatic brake for emergency use. The brake equipment incorporates the latest type of Westinghouse rubber-seated valves and O-ring packings for ease of maintenance. The brake cylinders, fitted with slack adjusters, are externally mounted on the bogie frame, and operation is through compensated clasp brake rigging. *(The leading and powered bogies were fitted with double, clasp type, brake blocks. Single brake blocks were fitted to all other wheels.)*

The permanent type of coupling between the coaches, which absorbs both buffing and drawing loads, has been designed to provide a smooth pick-up on starting and stable running at high speed. *(The couplings themselves can be described as being a solid buffing bar stretching the width of the carriage, and fastened to them at the sides by a conventional buffing arrangement. In the centre, the buffing bar was less thick than at the sides. The actual joining of the cars was above the buffing bar where a connection, bolted to the next vehicle, was made. The buffing gear can be seen in detail in the accompanying illustrations of the respective vehicle ends.)*

Normal coupling hooks, for emergency use, are in concealed *(folding)* recesses in the nose of each of the leading motor cars of the train. *(As built there was variation in the number of warning horns provided, for example, M60090 had two and M60093 three. The original fitting to the other power cars cannot be confirmed although it appears that as time passed all had the extra horn added.)*

These de-luxe trains have been built to the requirements of the British Transport Commission under the general direction of Mr JF Harrison, Chief Mechanical Engineer, British Railways Central Staff, in collaboration with Messrs SB Warder, Chief Electrical Engineer and F Grundy, Chief Traction Officer, and the Pullman Car Co Ltd. Mr AE Robson, Chief Mechanical & Electrical Engineer, London Midland Region, was responsible for inspection and for test running. Mr Jack Howe acted as consultant to the Metropolitan-Cammell Carriage & Wagon Co Ltd on passenger amenities and décor. Sub-contractors included the following:

Traction equipment: General Electric Co Ltd
NBL/MAN engines: North British Locomotive Co Ltd
Air-conditioning and lighting: J Stone & Co (Deptford) Ltd
Auxiliary engines: Rolls-Royce Ltd
Electro-pneumatic braking :Westinghouse Brake & Signal Co Ltd
Kitchen stoves: Radiation Ltd
Sink Units: James Scott & Co (Engineers) Ltd
Kitchen floor: laid by Durastic Ltd
Toilet commodes and basins: Twyfords Ltd
Bodyside door castings: Deans & Sons (Yorkshire) Ltd
Droplights (kitchen door): Etablissements Georges Klein et Cie
Droplights (Guard's door): Beckett, Laycock & Watkinson Ltd
Carpets (first class): S & J Stockwell & Co (Carpets) Ltd
Carpets (second class): Tomlinsons Ltd
Seat castings: GD Peters & Co Ltd
Seat cover materials: Edinburgh Weavers Ltd
PVC coverings (first class): Hunt & Winterbotham Ltd
PVC coverings (second class): ICI Ltd
Interior window units: Henry Hope & Sons Ltd

Venetian blinds (Crittal Solomatic type): Crittal Manufacturing Co Ltd
Plastic panels (saloon ceilings): Bakolite Ltd
Plastic panels (toilets): Holoplast Ltd
Interior timber partitions: Edmonton Panel Co Ltd
Body-shell insulation: JW Roberts Ltd
Interior insulation: W Gilmour Smith & Co Ltd
Ascot heaters: Ascot Gas & Water Heaters Ltd
Lavatory mosaic flooring: Carter & Co Ltd
Public address system: Clifford & Snell Ltd
Dunlopillo seat cushions: Dunlop Rubber Co Ltd
Springs: English Steel Springs Corporation Ltd
Axleboxes: Skefco Ball Bearing Co Ltd
Buffer springs: G Spencer Moulton & Co Ltd
Paint: Docker Bros Ltd
Engine/generator mountings, bogie bushes etc: Metalistik Ltd
Fire protection equipment: Graviner Manufacturing Co Ltd
Heat-demisters, driver's compartment: S Smith & Sons Ltd
Warning horns: Desilux Electrical Equipment Ltd
Windscreen wipers: Trico-Folberth Ltd
Buffers, hydro-pneumatic: George Turton Platts & Co Ltd
Pipe fittings: British Ermeto Corporation Ltd
Driver's and Guard's seats: AW Chapman Ltd
Metallic fittings, locks etc: J Beresford & Sons Ltd, Jones & Foster Ltd, J. Kaye & Sons Ltd, Taylor & Osbourne Ltd

In addition, there were a number of smaller subcontractors supplying minor items from both the UK and Europe.

Close up of the livery and crest detail. Due to possible confusion when boarding if the sets had been given fixed lettering, drop-in letters were used on both the LMR and WR. The WR staff booklet stated that, "trains divided into half sets for maintenance (are) allocated the numbers 4 through to 9. This number is carried on the solebar of the motor car second in the form of a small metal plate, with white lettering on a blue background. The number allocated will normally correspond with the last digit of the individual number of each vehicle forming the half-set", (none of these plates has been located on any of the photographs). (Pete Waterman/Just Like the Real Thing Collection)

Climbing through the Peak District and heading towards Chinley South Junction. George Behrend, commenting on the Midland Pullman, remarked, "A very restful and relaxing ride for the passenger, who is disturbed only by that pleasing and inevitable Pullman noise, the gentle tinkling of the spare crockery and cutlery on the tables." Behrend is one of the few not to have commented adversely on the ride. It was certainly not all luxury for the catering staff, as they were required to work for long periods, with some shifts extending to 12 hours. 1962 fares were reported as 69/- plus a 20/- supplement for a first-class single to Manchester, and 46/6 plus a 10/- supplement for a first-class single to Nottingham. By comparison the average weekly wage for an agricultural worker in the same year was 181/9d. (John Clarke)

Chapter 5

IN SERVICE ON THE LMR

The public service from Manchester commenced on the morning of 4th July 1960, using Set 2 with power car M60092 at the London end of the train. This set successfully maintained the service for the whole of the first week, arriving seven minutes early at St Pancras after the first up journey, although no doubt special care was taken to ensure that everything went to plan. The first down run back to Manchester that evening was presumably handled similarly, and it put on a spectacular display, covering the first 40 miles from St Pancras as far as Flitwick in just 32 minutes - a gain of almost six minutes in net running time. Additionally, the speed capability of the new sets, allowed them to breast the summit of the 1 in 119 Sharnbrook bank (between Bedford and Wellingborough) at 70 mph – a feat almost unheard of previously.

Nothing quite like these trains had ever been seen in the UK before, and with careful marketing, BR was quick to take advantage of the tremendous publicity they generated. Because of their appearance alone, the public could hardly miss the impact the new trains had; apart from leaflet and newspaper advertising, there was a special archway over the departure platform at St Pancras, and the livery was unique as well. Additionally, the LMR issued a chrome-litho poster in nine colours, based on a design by Mr AN Woolstenholme, and depicting a unit at speed through the Derbyshire countryside with the slogan:

The New
MIDLAND PULLMAN
First Class de-luxe travel – Supplementary fares
The last word in rail comfort
Limited accommodation, book in advance.

These were produced in volume, and were displayed, not just at stations on the route of the new trains, but anywhere on the system in the hope of attracting the attention of a wider audience. The posters also displayed the original timings of the new service, which was scheduled to depart from Manchester (Monday to Friday only) at 8.50am, pick up at Cheadle Heath at 9.04am, and arrive at St. Pancras at 12.03pm. The return journey left the capital at 6.10pm, stopping to set down at Cheadle Heath at 9.07pm, and arriving at Manchester Central at 9.21 pm. Information was also given about the lunchtime "fill-in" service for the set, the 12.45pm from St. Pancras to Leicester (London Road), arriving at 2.10 pm, from where after just a 23 minute turnaround, the train set off on its way back to London, arriving at 4.00pm. As one set was all that was required to operate the service, the spare set was kept at Derby, readily available should a problem occur with the set in use. Derby was just 60 miles from Manchester, but nearly 130 from St Pancras, and it is easy to see why the early decision to base the spare set Reddish (Manchester) was quickly revised, although it would remain the home depot for both sets throughout their life on the LMR. For the first few months of operation, a unit

was covering 578 miles daily including the Leicester turn.

The 132 first-class passengers were attended to by a staff of 14, excluding the operating staff of four: Driver, Second Driver, Guard and a travelling fitter. The use of second drivers is interesting, a further reference being made in 1964, although there is reason to believe that they were present from the outset on both the LMR and WR. It is likely that they were required at the insistence of the unions, due to the speed of the trains (unique at the time), and indeed, a similar arrangement prevailed for some years following the introduction of the HST sets. Likewise, it is believed (but cannot be confirmed) that the position of travelling fitter, a role referred to in more detail when dealing with the WR sets in the next chapter, remained constant throughout the life of the sets, one man being needed per set in service.

It is believed that both 6-car sets (for car numbers, see Appendix A) were delivered at the same time, but with one being (for now, at least) on permanent stand-by, maximum loadings would be required on most journeys to ensure any degree of profitability. The sets were rotated weekly, and because there was no weekend service, each set was in use for just five days out of every fourteen. Partly to facilitate swapping of half-sets, the trains were not given unit numbers, but instead relied on the power car and carriage numbers for identification. (This was in line with other regions, except the Southern Region, where its fleet of diesel-electric 3- and 6-car units carried both unit and vehicle number identification.) Also, be-

Three days before public running commenced and possibly a unique survivor from what was no doubt a VIP working. (The identity of Mr Noble has not been established, and his name does not appear in the list of the "godley" as was reproduced in the contemporary "Railway Gazette".) The original invitation was printed on a folded blue card which, when opened out as seen, measured just over 4 inches x 2 ½ inches. The reverse side was gold blocked on blue and included the words, "British Railways" and "Midland Pullman". The new Pullman crest previosuly referred to in this book will also be noted, but the associated scroling of the letters "LMR" could well be unique.

(Antony M Ford Collection)

57

St Pancras, believed to be around 1960. The nearest open door is that of the Guard's compartment, where a letter rack, coat hook, electric heaters and a foot warmer were provided. There were also various items of emergency equipment, including emergency hand-lamps, a crowbar, fire buckets, a ladder and a first-aid kit. No explanation has been found for the patch on the front of the unit. St Pancras was one of three locations on the LMR where a "shore-supply" was provided, the others being at Manchester Central and Reddish depot. Additionally, a "restricted shore-supply" (the term is not explained further) was available at Kentish Town Carriage Maintenance Depot (Cattle Dock Sidings) and also at Reddish.

cause the Pullmans were not (at this stage) equipped to work in multiple, no coupling code symbol was given. The maintenance of one half-set at a time enabled half a train to be available to cover as a spare if needed - a practice adopted on some foreign railways at the time. However, although the Pullman trains were split in two for maintenance, there is no evidence that the spare half-set was ever actually made available for such cover.

In order to appeal to the commuter, the schedule for the new service had to be fast, and at an average of just over 60mph each way, over a distance of just over 189 miles, it was — and indeed it was claimed to be the train with the fastest average speed at that time. In truth, however, some contemporary Eastern Region and Western Region services might legitimately have disputed this claim, but under the corporate BR banner, no-one was going to try to steal the thunder from the new service.

Where the new train certainly scored was in its power-to-weight ratio, compared with a conventional locomotive (steam or diesel) and its train. The new Midland Pullman 6-car set weighed 292 tons empty, say 310 tons fully laden, and this was a considerable improvement over a steam or diesel locomotive hauling an average 12-coach set, which might turn the scales in excess of 550 tons (albeit with a far greater passenger capacity). With a fixed formation, loadings are more predictable, and it follows that punctuality is easier to maintain. Comparisons at the time were being made to the relatively pedestrian steam schedules that still existed, and the difficulty came in attempting to fit a fast and reliable new service around a timetable where the predictability of steam-hauled freight trains, in particular, was difficult. A comment from David Blee, General Manager of the LMR, in a memorandum dated 12th July 1960, just a week after the train's introduction, was no doubt typical of the frustration that occurred at the time: "Timekeeping of the Mid-

Below: One of the earliest surviving brochures for the LMR service which commenced on 12th September 1960. Inside was a simple explanation of the facilities and service offered, which were also highlighted with three illustrations. On the back were details of the timings, with the information that bookings may also be made through stations, offices and official agencies. The whole was in plain blue with black and white illustrations.

(Antony M Ford Collection)

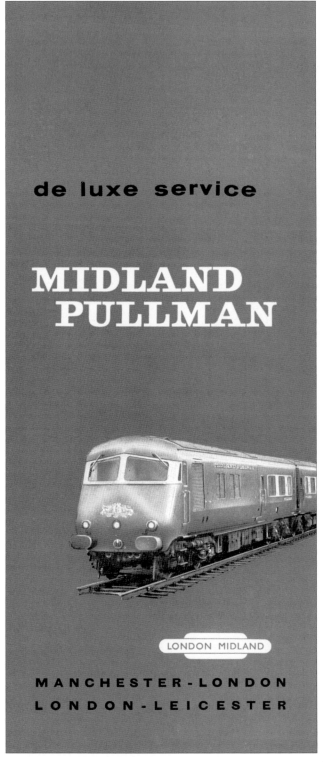

de luxe service

MIDLAND PULLMAN

LONDON MIDLAND

**MANCHESTER - LONDON
LONDON - LEICESTER**

EXPRESS SUCCESS!

MIDLAND PULLMAN
BRITAIN'S MOST EXCITING TRAIN

**MANCHESTER & LONDON
LONDON & LEICESTER,
LOUGHBOROUGH & NOTTINGHAM**

2nd October, 1961 until further notice
(except at Bank Holiday periods)

Above: A year later in 1961, a totally different approach was being taken with a much more eye-catching design. Again blue was used, but certainly not the "Nanking" blue shade, and black and orange had also appeared. The slogan on the rear, which appears to have been used only once, simply read, "Part of the new look of today's LONDON MIDLAND". Further publicity leaflets from the period are reproduced on pages 72 and 73.

(Ian Shawyer Collection)

North on the Midland main line in the early 1960s. For the passengers the noise levels were excellent, with only a sub-dued hum from the Rolls-Royce generator below the car. Scheduling was also very tight in places and required averages of over 80mph between Luton and Bedford, and 77mph over the 52 miles between Kettering and St Albans. However, with the rough riding characteristics that were well-reported, taking lunch could well have been a hazardous affair.

(Lewis Coles)

land Pullman MUST be maintained."

Blee's outburst resulted from a 12-minute delay to the new service caused by a signalman's error on the previous day in accepting the 8.50am Leicester-Wellingborough freight ahead of the up morning Pullman. It proved the point though; "one-offs", such as a Press run or the inaugural services, were possible even if they required considerable effort on the part of numerous members of staff, and this had been proved with the early arrivals of both up and down services just eight days earlier. However, a beleaguered man on the ground, pressured no doubt by Control, the timetable and train crews, could be forgiven for getting it wrong, and the signalman in question was undoubtedly just one example. Similar situations no doubt occurred on countless other occasions, but as time passed, perhaps the General Manager was not always informed, or even interested.

Not all difficulties were preventable, as on 27th July 1960, just over three weeks after the new service had commenced, a tyre worked loose on the fifth vehicle of

the set in use (the exact vehicle and set are not identified). The situation could have been disastrous, and the report calmly states that, "a fire was caused as a result of the tyre dragging on the adjacent brake block. This was extinguished by the crew, after which the train continued at the reduced speed of 60mph". It is recorded that the tyres on all the cars were subsequently changed, but it is not known whether the sets were withdrawn until the work had been carried, nor how the WR sets were affected. Presumably, they were similarly modified, or at least checked (if so, it would have been before they entered public service). The subject of tyres will come up again later in this chapter.

Notwithstanding this incident (which appears not to have attracted any adverse Press reaction) it might be expected that the first weeks of operation would be a honeymoon period as far as loadings were concerned. In fact, it was destined to be a somewhat long honeymoon as, according to railway figures, loadings were consistently high and were rarely less than 100 passengers per trip.

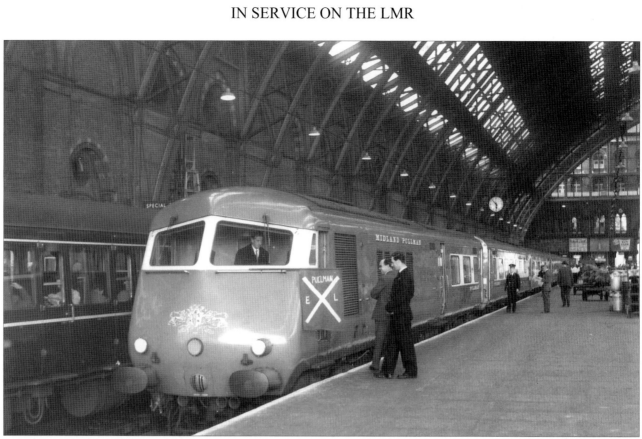

St Pancras again, and with the time at 5.50 pm, the Manchester service is almost ready for its scheduled 6.10pm departure north. The flag indicates that the set must not be moved due to the presence of a maintenance crew underneath. It was originally stated that the service times were experimental and could be reviewed later, and indeed this did happen for the morning departure from Manchester, where pressure from business men led to an earlier departure time of 7.45am from 2nd January 1961. The earlier arrival at the Capital was a profitable move, as the previous 9.00am departure was considered too late for breakfast, and with arrival in London scheduled for mid-day, too early for luncheon as well. The evening departure remained unaltered for the life of the service and was, as would be expected, heavily orientated towards the service of food. (S Creer)

Apart from ticket receipts, catering sales were also good, and although the following was written some time later in 1963, most of the principles applied from the outset: "Although not all morning passengers eat breakfast, practically everyone has dinner in the evening…since the most miserly passenger finds it near-impossible to sit hungry in a coach full of feeders."

At this time the decision was made to continue with a full cooking service on board, rather than the original proposal for pre-packaged food, and there was much scope for imagination by the chefs themselves. The staff worked long hours, and an article in *Modern Railways* for July 1963 lucidly described the conditions in the kitchen cars at that time:

"It is a long day for the chefs (two catering vehicles per six coach set) and their assistants. Departing from Manchester at 7.45am, they may each serve a dozen or so full breakfasts and a number of continental breakfasts and cups of coffee. On the down Nottingham there may be 30 passengers, of whom perhaps twelve may order lunch (many having lunch appointments at their destinations); the return from Nottingham at 3.30pm, brings light catering demands for teas and pots of tea. The heavy

duties of the day come with the 6.10pm down to Manchester, when each chef may have to serve almost all of his 60 or so passengers with dinner. Arrival in Manchester at 9.20pm ends a 13hr 35min tour of duty. Each crew member has one working day off in five; the relief chef takes over each of the duties of each of the regular train's crew of four in turn, and thus has one day in five free himself. The cooking staff appreciate the train's speed and smoothness in acceleration and deceleration; they greatly dislike its occasional exuberance in riding."

It was all good economic news for BR, although not all figures relating to the trains have been found. It was officially reported in November 1960 that the Manchester service would bring in an estimated surplus over expenditure of £46,000 annually, presumably after depreciation costs were allowed for (although, at this stage, this amount was not stated). Other papers refer to a 16.5% profit on cost for the Midland Pullman between July and November 1960.

Because of inflation, it is risky to quote actual fares four decades later, but as an example, the basic first-class single fare between Manchester Central and St Pancras by Blue Pullman was then £3 9s (£3.45), but added to

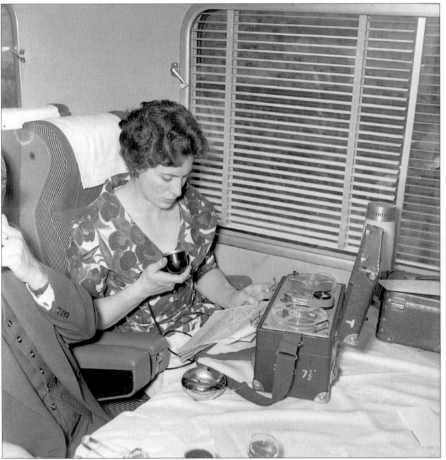

Contemporary business class travel of the 1960s. Presumably taken to illustrate the ease with which the busy executive could conduct work on the train, the photograph includes a dictating machine of the period – the days of audio typing. This style of view was used to woo potential passengers in the advertising brochures of the day.

Above: Even the sugar cubes had their own Pullman wrapper – blue and white, of course!
(Antony M Ford Collection)

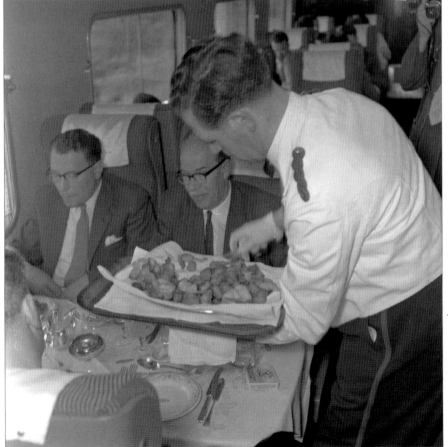

Another form of illustration used in advertising brochures, highlighting, not unnaturally, the standard of service. Here conductor Chris Lade is supposedly serving passengers, although this particular view is known to have also been posed. Note the second cameraman just visible top right. Apart from the food, a packet of Players' cigarettes can also be seen on the table. The gentleman seated to the left would appear to be identical to the passenger depicted on Page 29, top-right.

Australian Test Cricket Captain, Richie Benaud, at the controls at St Pancras prior to the Australia team travelling to Manchester for the Fourth Test at Old Trafford, which began on 27th July 1961. (Australia went on to win the Test by 54 runs and the series 2-1.)

Below: The plate displayed at the barrier at Manchester Central indicating the morning up service, now on display at the National Railway Museum.
(Howard Sprenger)

THE 7:45
MIDLAND
PULLMAN

FIRST CLASS
ONLY

PLEASE SHOW
TICKETS

this was the Pullman supplement of £1, and meals were a further, optional expense; from Cheadle Heath there was a saving of 9d on the basic fare only. Allowing for the Pullman supplement, this was slightly higher than the comparable weekday BEA ticket for a flight between Manchester and London, which was set at £4 1s (£4.05). The air journey also took 30 to 40 minutes less, even allowing for the time it took to get to and from the airports. (Average wages of the period were little more than £8 to £10 weekly, so both services were out of the reach of the most people.) Pitching the service at the business community, and charging higher fares as a result, had been a gamble, but it was one that appears to have paid off handsomely.

However, on the train itself, there were already the first rumblings of discontent, initially over the ride. A reference in the surviving records at the National Archive refers to correspondence on the ride quality between the manufacturers, the LMR and BRB as early as 5th September 1960, at which time the train had been in service for just nine weeks. Unfortunately, the actual file of papers referred to appears not to have survived. It also appears that comments were made by passengers about the fittings in the vehicles, which culminated in letters to both the Railway and the National Press. One letter to *The Guardian* from a Miss Campbell commented that it was neces-

sary to adopt a "contorted crab movement" in order to gain access to the inside window seat. The reply from BR was slightly tongue-in-cheek: "seats are moveable so as to ensure that those who have no wish to indulge in the kind of movement Miss Campbell describes, are not constrained to do so".

Reports of poor riding were soon to reach the notice of JF Harrison, the CME for BR, who was also no doubt aware of complaints such as that above. He penned an internal note about the sets, although unfortunately only the last page survives, on which this final paragraph is written, "I am not dealing with the various comments that the public have such a lot of time to write about, such as train seats, etc, because it is all a matter of personal opinion, and anyone who travels by air and does not complain, compared with travelling in the Blue Train, wants their head examined".

The poor riding might have contributed to a revision of the train loadings that was noted in the *Daily Telegraph* during October 1960. Here it was stated that the passenger loadings were less than 60%, a figure that is totally at odds with the 100 passengers per trip figure quoted by BR. (BR's figure translates to a 76% loading, and the percentage given in the Press represented a passenger loading of just 79 persons. Care should be taken with these figures as there is no indication as to exactly what the Press were referring to; the Midland Pullman service to and from Manchester only, the addition of loadings on the mid-day "fill-in" turn, or loadings with the WR trains by then also running.)

Initially, suspicion about the riding problems again centred on the shock absorbers, based on the fact that one was found to have broken in August 1960. As a result, all dampers were replaced on the stand-by 6-car and running trials were carried out. The surviving paperwork also contains a note, "Dampers made by Messrs Armstrong", but it is not clear whether this referred to the new items or those that had been replaced, or both. An additional problem was a fractured brake block that was discovered around the same time, although happily, this was a one-off incident. (This is not thought to be to the same incident involving the tyre mentioned earlier.)

Despite the replacement of the dampers, there was continuing disquiet from the travelling public, and also by now, the train staff. It was enough to goad BR into more tests, which for the first time it is believed, involved the embryonic Research Department at Derby. Accordingly Set 2 was used for riding trials in both directions between Derby and Leicester on 2nd December 1960, which involved displacement measurement tests of the first six bogies (ie, the first three vehicles) of the unit. It was found that the leading bogie of the power car (M60092) gave a very poor vertical ride, and that the first bogie of the third vehicle (parlour car M60742, over which there appear to have been more complaints generally than any other vehicle) was poor in the lateral direction. However observers on board, who were regular travellers on the train, commented that, "it was better than usual"! At about the same time, additional riding tests were also carried out on what later became the BR test track at Old Dalby. Further tests were made between Derby and Leicester in January 1961, this time involving Set 1. No mention is made of these results, but they were probably broadly similar to those previously obtained.

The results that were published were not unexpected, being heavy on obvious fact, but short on specific solutions. The main conclusions were that the vertical ride over the leading bogie of the power car was poor, the comfort riding factor being within a range of 1.5 to 4.7 at

speeds between 50 and 90mph (the accepted minimum comfort level was 6). The remaining bogies, however, gave a better vertical ride than the BR standard double-bolster bogie when these latter items were fitted with new tyres. It was also stated that hunting occurred on at least two of the bogies at 80mph and over, which itself led to a riding factor below 6 at this speed.

Apart from the damper replacement, there was little else of any substance done improve matters, but variously-sized pieces of rubber were incorporated in an attempt to reduce knocks and banging. The vertical movement affecting the leading bogie of the power car was also transmitted to the trailing end of the vehicle, with the result that knowledgeable travellers avoided the power car, and instead, obtained a seat midway along a vehicle. Even so, continuing letters of complaint from the public expressed fears of a derailment, so Derby suggested fitting CCTV cameras to the bogies, so that their behaviour could be observed at speed. While this would have been a technological innovation for the period, it does not appear to have been carried out.

OS Nock, in his regular performance articles in the *Railway Magazine,* reported on several runs with the sets, both on the LMR and WR. Initially, in 1960 he had waxed lyrical about the trains, and when commenting on a cab ride from Manchester, did nothing but sing their praises. Three years later, though, he had almost completely changed his tune, likening the ride to "a peculiar shuddering". Nevertheless, he made an attempt at a balanced view, and reminded the reader that his preference for loco-hauled Pullmans might have been based on a rosy memory. His final statement, however, was a damming criticism. Having mentioned that his preference for loco-hauled Pullmans had been reinforced while the sets were away for overhaul, he concluded, "Now, alas, the blue train is back and continuing its purgatorial progress". To be fair, many contemporary DMUs were equally uncomfortable at speed, but the Pullman, despite its greater cushioning of human anatomy, travelled faster, and this cushioning could not make up for its undoubted pitfalls.

It has to be admitted that patronage on the Leicester turn was poor, with only 12 to 15 passengers on the train at times, so accordingly, the decision was taken to

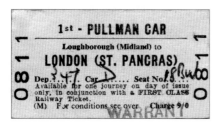

First class tickets from the LMR operation, all of the period 1964/5. Colouring was a light buff with black lettering.

(Antony M Ford Collection)

The down mid-day, fill-in turn arriving at Leicester (London Road). It has been suggested that the later mid-day Nottingham service might have sometimes travelled out via Leicester, returning via Manton. Reporting numbers were 1D08 for the 11.15am St Pancras to Nottingham and 1C71 for the 3.30pm return working.   *(D Stubbs)*

extend the service though to Nottingham from January 1961, which coincided with an earlier morning departure from Manchester at 7.45am from the 2nd of that month, and hence, an earlier arrival at St. Pancras. It was hoped this would improve loadings on the fill-in turn, and with a greater distance to cover in the middle of the day, the lunchtime departure from St Pancras was brought forward to 11.15am, but the quick turnaround at the new destination, resulting in a 3.30pm departure from Nottingham, meant that as with the earlier Leicester service, the train was unlikely to see the same clientele in both directions on the same day.

The lunchtime fill-in turns were also affected by an ongoing labour dispute over the staffing and cleaning of the trains (simply put, "who cleaned what?"), which really had its roots elsewhere. The NUR represented existing BR restaurant car staff, and was fearful that the new trains were an extension of private enterprise on what was a State-run system. In their eyes, BR was condoning private enterprise by promoting the new service. What the NUR seems to have failed to grasp was that, since June 1954, the BTC had been the owners of the whole of the equity in the Pullman Car Co, although there was £386,000 of Preference Stock outstanding, the holders of

which, while being guaranteed a dividend, had no voting rights. An added difficulty was that the Pullman Car Co still had a Board of Directors, who administered the Pullman staff, and who, in turn, had different rates of pay and conditions from the BR staff who worked for the British Transport Hotels & Catering Service.

The union felt that the situation could, at best, mean the relegation of existing restaurant car staff working between London and Manchester to less remunerative services, or at worst, redundancy. This was initially solved by sending BR staff to work the new trains, albeit under Pullman staff guidance (the word "supervision" is deliberately not used) and also by amalgamating grades, rates of pay and lines of promotion. While this enabled the Midland main line service to begin running, the union was still far from happy over what they perceived as a service run by private enterprise.

At the time of their introduction, staffing was by BR restaurant car staff, with five additional Pullman men working on a temporary basis to help to establish the service. These included a Conductor, a Senior Chef and three Senior Attendants, who were in charge of stock levels on the train.

Meanwhile, the Pullman Car Co was advertising

Drivers posed for the photographer in 1960; the uniform of footplate staff on the LMR was a Navy blue battledress. Initially, the crew for the daily service came from Kentish Town and would work double-home to Manchester, returning with the morning service the next day, with the set being serviced at Reddish overnight. Regretfully the names of these men as with those opposite were not recorded.

for additional staff from the Manchester area, which they were later able to recruit. The NUR had intended to draw attention to its grievance by the withdrawal of its labour from all BR restaurant cars from 4th January, which, it will be recalled, was the intended start date for the Midland line service. BR management had to consider their next moves very carefully in order to avoid attracting adverse publicity to the new service.

There followed an unhappy truce between all sides until, amid much Press advertising, the announcement was made over the proposed extension of the midday service from Leicester to Nottingham, with effect from 2nd January 1961, whereupon the threat of industrial action resulted in a postponement of the revision for some months. It appears that BR had failed to recall its own consent from early 1960 not to extend Pullman services, and Leicester to Nottingham was clearly such an extension. In addition to the simmering of discontent over perceived private enterprise operation, there was another grumble from BR staff on loan being required to wear standard Pullman numerical badge identification. Yet another concern was over duties, with BR restaurant car staff on loan refusing to handle soiled linen on the trains, and stating that this was not part of an attendant's task.

The Nottingham service did eventually start as described, but it did not become fully-operational until as late as 2nd October 1961, having in the interim suffered periods of temporary withdrawal, curtailment at Leicester, and a lack of a meal service beyond that point. The latter was due to the somewhat bizarre situation whereby on reaching Leicester, the entire seconded BR catering staff "downed cutlery" and went on strike – but only as far as Nottingham and back to Leicester, during which time they retired en masse to the kitchens. With such a limited patronage, it is likely that very few hungry and thirsty passengers even noticed.

In order to facilitate seating in accordance with the seat reservations made for the return journey, Pullman clerical staff (who were not in any way party to the dispute) travelled on the train daily to collect the reservations chart at Nottingham, and allocate seats to any late-coming passengers, who had arrived without reservations. At Leicester, the Train Conductor and attendants would reappear as mentioned. None of this though would have assisted in endearing the midday train to its potential customers.

There was none of the bad feeling that typified the bitter public disagreements so common a few years later, and the whole situation was summed up in a cartoon from the *Daily Mail* (a copy of which was pinned up in at least one of the kitchen cars) in which a railwayman was shown commenting on the dispute: "Unofficially this is an

Two crews recorded at the same time, possibly with a bowler-hatted locomotive inspector. Initially, ten men were in the Pullman link, which still included some regular steam working as late as 1962. Incidentally, the blue and white colour of the new trains also matched the colours used by the Pullman Car Co for their own staff uniforms after WWII. Stewards were also issued with special Midland Pullman badges, together with white gloves soon after the service commenced, although these do not appear to be in use in the photographs.

official dispute. But officially this is an unofficial dispute". When it was finally resolved, it was agreed that the Pullman Car Co, who up to that time had advertised their own vacancies, would offer them to existing restaurant car staff, and that these men's seniority would be protected if it was later necessary for them to return to their former role. Additionally, it allowed for some BR staff to wear identical Pullman uniforms on non-Pullman services.

This was an unhappy period in labour-relations, which did neither side any good, but was not helped by a BR spokesman using the choice words, "there is some substance to their claim". It is worth mentioning at this point that the later introduction of the Pullman service on the Western Region involved a similar mixed level of staffing, but any disputes over staffing levels relative to the Pullman Car Co would have been meaningless by this time as it was fully vested in BR in 1962.

The limited use of the sets during the day meant there was plenty of time for maintenance and cleaning (both external and internal), this aspect being considered of paramount importance for keeping up the standard of the prestige service. Cleaning occupied much of the initial 2hr 20min layover at St Pancras following the midday fill in turn. Unfortunately, the manufacturers who supplied the external paint had advised that it was more suited to hand washing rather than an automated carriage washing plant, with the result that the hand washing occupied a considerable part of the layover time, as well as being labour-intensive and costly. Initially, the cleaning was undertaken at St. Pancras, but when the service was

extended to Nottingham, the work was transferred there. How long such a disciplined regime continued is not reported, but it appears from the *Modern Railways* article of July 1963 that it was still being done at least up until that time - an indication perhaps, that the Blue Pullmans were still considered to be the jewels in the crown three years after their introduction. Paul Metcalfe, in his excellent article on the trains in *Classic Diesels & Electrics* refers to the "Manchester Experiment", where fares were reduced by a third in an attempt to increase passenger numbers. However, this does not agree with the reports of consistent loadings previously mentioned.

Servicing was usually carried out at night, and involved two electrical fitters and two mates scheduled as follows: a daily check taking 2 to 4 hours, a weekly check taking 5 hours, and every five weeks, a 22-hour check. The total servicing time each night, involving all staff, which probably included cleaners as well, was seven hours per set (the weekly and five-weekly checks were usually carried out at weekends). It is not known whether these service intervals were modified later in the life of the trains. An external starter button was fitted to the vehicles carrying the auxiliary Rolls-Royce engines so that they could be checked even if the vehicle was locked.

Meanwhile, despite pressure from the management of the LMR over timekeeping, the service rapidly deteriorated as the novelty apparently wore off. This may have been partly due to the poor riding, and it is interesting to speculate whether the staff might have deliberately slowed down the service at times, for their own sake and that of the fare paying passengers, as it cannot have been

pleasant at speed at the front end (although arguably no worse than on many steam engines).

By the end of 1960, only 65% of the services were running within 5 minutes of "right-time", compared with 90% when the service was introduced. However, a year later, the 15th December 1961 issue of *The Railway Gazette* included a brief paragraph under their regular "Notes and News" feature: "Success of Midland Pullman. The London Midland Region of British Railways has announced that the Midland Pullman is attracting an average loading of 95 per cent capacity, and has a record of 95 per cent punctuality". Perhaps, in reality, the truth was somewhere between the two extremes.

Not in doubt is the fact that, on the LMR, the highest loadings were achieved on the Manchester service, and the daily fill-in to and from Leicester and Nottingham was known to have attracted scant patronage. (According to *Modern Railways*, the disadvantage with the fill-in turn was that passengers objected to paying a supplement over what was a relatively short distance. This view by a well-respected magazine is difficult to believe, as the distance between St Pancras to Leicester or Nottingham is comparable with that covered by the Bournemouth Belle, and far greater than that covered by the Brighton Belle. In both these cases, there was never any objection to the supplement charged.)

With the introduction of 4-digit train identification on BR, the morning departure from Manchester became 1C43 from 12th June 1961, while the 3.30pm from Nottingham was classified as 1C71. In the down direction, the designations were, 1D0H for the 11.15am to Nottingham, and 1H20 for the 6.10pm from St. Pancras.

1962 also started with an unfortunate incident that could so nearly have resulted in tragedy. On 1st February, the down lunchtime service to Leicester ran over, at high speed, a permanent way jack, that had been left by workmen in the "four-foot" near the south end of Haverstock Tunnel. The result was stated to be "considerable damage to the underneath of the train" although, fortunately, it kept to the rails. The service was terminated at West Hampstead with passengers transferring to an ordinary service for the remainder of their journey.

An 0-6-0 "Jinty" tank engine was later used to pull the set to Cricklewood for repairs, but on being examined, the damage must also have been found to be less than first feared, as the same set was able to take up its booked working back to Manchester that evening. This incident was an interesting repeat of one on the Western Region, where one of its sets had suffered an identical incident near Swindon just a few weeks earlier on 5th December. On that occasion, only the fuel tank was damaged, and the set was towed to Swindon Works for repair.

Meanwhile, despite attempts at advertising, Nottingham was soon realised to be a poor choice from which to attract revenue, and this added to questions being asked about having one set on permanent standby, covering what was little more than a single return run to Manchester daily.

Accordingly, the LMR cast its eyes elsewhere for places where revenue might be gained, and one of the obvious choices was Liverpool. A thorough feasibility study was carried out over some months, with much of the work being undertaken by the Manchester Line Manager, and the conclusion reached was that a second daily service was very likely to be feasible, working a diagram that would involve departure from St Pancras at 7.45am, picking up at Luton at 8.12am, and then running via Manchester (arrive 11.05am) and Warrington (11.23am) to reach Liverpool at 11.45am. A midday fill-in was also envisaged just between Liverpool and Manchester. It was later suggested to put the St Pancras departure back to 8.00am, with a corresponding alteration to the other times, to give passengers from elsewhere (particularly from the SR) easier access to the train. The return journey would be from Liverpool at 5.45pm, with the same stops so as to arrive at St Pancras at 9.40pm. The estimate was for an average 80% loading on the second, Liverpool, train. Clearly though this would involve both Blue Pullman sets operating daily and with no stand-by available, discussion took place with the SR about having a spare set of loco-hauled Pullman coaches available if necessary. (These would have been vehicles from the former Golden Arrow service which, by this time, was already no longer restricted to just Pullman vehicles.)

The Blue Pullman set for the Liverpool service would be dealt with at a new servicing depot at Allerton, which would be equipped like Cricklewood. Reddish, however, would remain the home depot for both sets, and this is where more major work would be carried out. Five ex-SR Pullman cars were subsequently sent to Etches Park carriage sidings at Derby. These were two brake vehicles, Athene and Fortuna, a parlour car, Ceteia, and two kitchen cars, Thetis, and Thalia. With the exception of the first two, they eventually found their way into the WR "Wells Fargo" spare set mentioned in Appendix A.

The LMR Board, however, decided not to proceed with the Liverpool service. Publicly, this was because of the impending electrification of the West Coast Main Line, but it is perhaps more likely that the complaints of poor riding had not diminished, and it was felt that a restraint on the expansion of services was necessary until the difficulties had been resolved (after all, why create another source of complaint?). In the event, of course, the poor riding was never fixed.

Opposite: 0-6-0T No 47449 propelling the failed mid-day Pullman service back into Cricklewood Depot on 1st February 1962, following the incident at Haverstock Tunnel. Subsequent examination revealed that only parts of the air-conditioning system were affected. Despite the importance of the various servicing facilities (Cricklewood, Reddish, Old Oak Common, etc) few photographs have been located of the trains at these establishments. Notwithstanding the comment within the text about hand washing, carriage-washing facilities also existed at Reddish and Kentish Town, and it is believed these were used as required. *(A Swain)*

M60093 at St Pancras, still with the same dent as was noted on page 37, although at least now the wipers are more correctly parked!

Considering that the Manchester service was still operating successfully, the decision not to go ahead with the Liverpool service can be considered slightly surprising in view of the good business case that had been prepared for the utilisation of an expensive and depreciating asset, that was otherwise earning nothing. Perhaps in the genuine belief that the service was about to be approved, or maybe just to spur the LMR Board into action, the Manchester Line Manager began publicising the new service with a proposed start from the autumn 1963 timetable. (The long lead-time was considered necessary in order to have the necessary servicing infrastructure in place, amongst other things.) The announcement was picked up and reported in a number of newspapers, as well as contemporary railway magazines, but the effect was perhaps the opposite to what the Line Manager expected. He was given a mild rebuke, and told to advise all concerned that the service would not now commence.

Unfortunately, while the LMR Board might have considered that the Liverpool service was purely a proposal, there were those on the Mersey who were less than satisfied with the decision, especially in view of the publicity already given. An article in the *Liverpool Daily Post* for 23rd August 1962 had the headline, "Progress marches backwards on Liverpool-London line". It was accompanied by a publicity photograph of a 6-car Blue

Opposite: The 7.45am ex-Manchester Central approaching Bedford (Midland Road) on a misty 18th September 1961. A year earlier, it was reported that during the initial week of operation, the first up service was seven minutes early arriving in London, while in the same week, all the down trains managed the first 40 miles from St Pancras in 32 minutes; no doubt there was some assistance by the operators in achieving this. The same report refers to the fact that the train was, on average, 4 to 8 minutes early every day (in which direction is not stated) but only on the first four days. What happened on fifth day? The 3hr 13min timing between Manchester and St Pancras was the fastest since before 1914, when the best had been 3hr 35min. In order to maintain this speed, some of the diesel drivers would run at 95mph or even 100mph to keep time, this despite the fact that even with all the modern technology incorporated in the trains, there was no AWS on the units operating over the Midland main line until 1962. Accordingly, the sets would have been operated on full power for much of the time in order to maintain the schedule, and should an engine fail, the schedule would inevitably suffer. Fortunately, this did not happen often, and they are recalled as being reliable units. (Michael Mensing)

Left: Advertising, this time to apply from 1ˢᵗ January 1962, including the Leicester and Nottingham workings. Compared with the brochure depicted on page 59, the departure time from Manchester has been changed to 7.45am, the reason for which is described on page 65. The single fare referred to as applying in 1961 has also risen to 63/6d, although the supplement is unaltered.

Centre: 1961 publicity material, this time with three-colour printing: red, black, and of course blue. Inside is a description and two photographs, the "passengers" are those seen in the lower view on page 62 again, but this time being served by a different steward. Fares are also given as Manchester to London single at 57/6d, plus a 20/- Pullman supplement. Meals, of course, were additional. Simpler "pocket" advertising, without illustrations, was also produced in the same year.

Far right: A direct approach to the non-business class market, possibly aimed partly at the American tourist market. (This would be exactly the same as the Western Region's Oxford Pullman service of 1967, which is referred to in the next chapter.) The leaflet here incorporates a number of quotes, the principal component of which was an article from "The Daily Telegraph" of 27ᵗʰ July 1960 which reported on the favourable comments made by a delegation of American railway executives. "They agreed that the finest train they had seen abroad was the new Pullman which is to be placed in service between London and Manchester". The quote continued, "We were particularly impressed by the interior decoration and the speed". "The seating was comfortable and the lighting excellent and the air-conditioning good. We found the kitchens very well planned and we had food on our trial run". Perhaps even Metropolitan-Cammell had wooed the overseas visitors in the hope of an export order.

(All Antony M Ford Collection)

Below: This time the point of the brochure was a five minute acceleration, which applied from 10th September 1962. This meant that arrival at St Pancras from Manchester was now scheduled for 10.55am. There was however, no corresponding alteration in the return journey times. The single fare between Manchester and London had also risen again, this time to 69/-. Notice on the front the reference to "London Midland Railway", was this intentional or a designers slip?

Above: Finally, some publicity material from September 1963. This time, the alteration in the fare structure was slightly downwards - but only in favour of passengers to and from Cheadle Heath who would save 1/6d compared with 1962. This particular brochure opened out to four folds and included a number of "toned" views, such as the one seen above. Blue and white were of course used, but also, and perhaps surprisingly, a shade of olive green.

(All Antony M Ford Collection)

Numerically, the first of the power cars, M60090, on display at the Derby Works Open Day on 15th August 1964; the coupling cover is open. From its freshly-painted appearance, the set might be fresh from overhaul with the provision of electrification warning flashes apparently being the only addition from new. *(Antony M Ford)*

Pullman set together with the caption, "The train that could provide additional passenger accommodation over the main line through Matlock". It took a private meeting between BR and (it was stated) "journalists from Liverpool" to resolve the situation, after which nothing else appears to have been mentioned. To be fair, the Liverpool Press did have a point; in 1962, their best service to London took 4hr 5min, compared to 3hr 20min in 1939. The proposed Pullman service would have been 3hr 55min down, and four hours in the up direction, but at least it would have been in luxury! Somehow the local press had not picked up the fact that timings would not be improved, yet the existing schedule appeared to be their main gripe. It would take electrification a few years later for honour to be satisfied.

This was not the last idea to extend the usage of the trains, as there was also a preliminary discussion (privately within BR) about a luxury service between either Manchester or Liverpool and Glasgow. Again, the rough riding, together with a later BR view that the life of the sets was limited, pending electrification, forestalled this idea.

Before leaving the topic of projected services, it should be mentioned that Charles Long, in his May 1973 article in *Railway World*, commented that in relation to the Liverpool service, "basically, it was lack of agreement with the unions on staffing that prevented the introduction of a London-based Midland Pullman using the stand-by 6-car diesel unit". To some extent, however, he also contradicted himself slightly further on in the article when he made the following very interesting point:

"Perhaps it is not widely known that late in 1962, a group of eight pre-war Pullmans were transferred from the Southern to the London Midland in anticipation of such a service to cover failures in traffic and routine maintenance periods. Because of weight restrictions laid down by operating authorities, the proposed traffic formation was, in fact, no more than five cars, and, in order to provide a seating capacity equivalent to the diesel units, the vehicles selected (although all nominally first-class) were a mixed bag of traditional-style firsts, with massive armchairs 1+1 each side of the central gangway, and former seconds which, while being refurbished internally, retained a 2+1 fixed-seating layout. In keeping with former Pullman practice, the ex-seconds were all named when "up-classed". The names chosen (Ceteia, Hebe, Melandra, Thalia, Thesis) had a strong classical flavour and were drawn from a list suggested by the London Midland. After some ten years, I cannot recall all the rejected names, but one does stick in the memory - Terpsichore. Not surprisingly, the Pullman management felt it would not be appropriate for a railway vehicle to commemorate the Greek Muse of dancing!"

It is not thought that the stand-by set was ever needed on the Midland line, but it later found a use on the WR, and the subject of the use of these vehicles for the first time is covered in the next chapter.

With both sets involved in maintenance and modification in 1962, had there been a will to provide the Liverpool service, perhaps it could even have commenced using the stand-by loco-hauled set, but this would hardly have conjured up the image required. Additionally, the union dispute over the Nottingham extension was still going on, and with the new Liverpool train having to run beyond Manchester, this could have been seen as displaying a "blue" flag to a bull.

It would appear surprising that the LMR went to the expense of preparing a spare set of loco-hauled vehicles unless it felt there was likely to be a definite need for them. Perhaps even the union dispute was just an excuse, and it should be stated here that no information has been located about any proposal for an additional 6-car Blue Pullman rake at this time to act as a spare set, although this is perhaps understandable.

In a narrative such as this, it is easy to jump ahead in time to cover all aspects of a particular topic, and it is now necessary to return to mid-1961, when despite any problems over ride quality, the trains were still viewed with public pride by the LMR. Euston, therefore, entered into an agreement whereby a chauffeur service operated by Messrs Victor Britain Ltd provided luxury motor vehicles to meet passengers arriving off the up Manchester service, and take them on the final leg of their journey to their London destinations. It was hoped by all concerned (although presumably not by the drivers of the famous black-cabs) that the clientele from the Pullman would favour such a service, and discussions took place from 18th May 1961. Evidently, they were quickly concluded, for the new arrangement commenced as early as 5th June 1961. Publicity was provided by advertising cards that were handed to each passenger on board the train.

Unfortunately the take up was not as good as had been expected, and with an average patronage of just one person a week, it was inevitable that the service would be withdrawn. No actual date is given for this, but is was unlikely to have been protracted. Interestingly, the same car firm had successfully operated a similar service some years earlier, it is believed from Paddington, but it eventually suffered a similar fate.

In the same year, 1961, there was a suggestion to use a Pullman set from Leicester to London in connection with Leicester City's appearance in the FA Cup Final (a final that they were to lose 2-0 to Tottenham Hotspur). However, nothing came of the suggestion on the basis of limited demand, together with the high number of ordinary specials already running from Leicester on that day.

Returning to the ride quality, by late-1961 complaints had not diminished as BR might have hoped, but instead, were increasing. It is perhaps surprising that during the adverse publicity over the abortive Liverpool ser-

vice, no mention of ride quality was referred to, even though it was well known by then. One of the earliest public letters of complaint appeared in the *Manchester Evening Chronicle* as early as August 1960, under the heading "With a Splash". The letter criticised the ride quality and was signed, "A disgruntled Manchester Businessman".

BR, though, were hardly naïve regarding the behaviour of their latest prestige service, and on this occasion, a more technical approach appears to been made in a genuine attempt to resolve matters once and for all. Accordingly, the bogies on one set (which one is not known) were modified at Derby Works with long swing links and torsion bars that at first appeared to offer a vast improvement. The second set was similarly modified in July 1962, after which, on 20th August 1962, further riding assessments were carried out using a "delegation" of BR staff, who were themselves regular travellers on the service. The results were, frankly, disappointing for it was noted that the initial improvement had not been maintained. Whilst at Derby in 1962, both sets also received "heavy maintenance".

The August 1962 riding assessments were carried out on the regular public service between St Pancras and Leicester, which was the section over which the Midland Pullman achieved its fastest average speed. All three types of vehicle forming the 6-car sets were assessed, and it was reported that, although the motor bogies were reasonable, the trailing bogies appeared to have deteriorated since the report writer's previous trip in May 1962, and indeed, they were now giving the occasional metallic knock. (This time the converse of what was generally held appears for the first time – usually the trailers were better than the motored vehicles!) It was also admitted there was some difficulty in eating and drinking, and some passengers were overheard in conversation stating that they would not take lunch, as is was impossible to eat soup or drink coffee at speed. No doubt from personal observation at the time, the writer continued, "Indeed lunch was quite a hazardous business…almost impossible to write this at speed."

Overall, the report concluded that the ride was generally very jerky, and it was suggested that despite the motor bogies being better than the trailer bogies, it would be worth checking the roundness of the tyres. It was again suggested that CCTV be used on the bogies, and again this appears to have been ignored. Further evidence about the poor riding was also sent to BR from the Pullman Car Co, including several letters from passengers who appeared genuinely fearful that the vehicles would derail. These daily complaints did not go unnoticed by the train staff either, as at some stage, an internal memorandum (normally reserved for completion by crew members only) was distributed to passengers, who were invited to pass comment on the ride. Understandably such an action did not meet with much favour with the LMR Board.

The most serious difficulty to date was reported on

20th September 1962, and is said to have occurred within the previous two months. It involved a fractured leading bogie tyre, and might then give some credence to the suggestion regarding the roundness of the tyres, but it could also have been a result of the continual knocking that the tyres were subjected to as a result of the bogie behaviour. The immediate outcome was that all tyres on both sets were changed immediately, and this was done at Derby. After this, there does not appear to have been a similar problem again, and it is reasonable to assume that the same components on the WR sets were similarly checked, but this is not reported anywhere. It was also stated that a spare bogie had been used for experiments into ride quality at this time, and it would be interesting to know more details about this.

The same report mentioned problems with the main generators reducing their output due to an insulation breakdown, and the hydraulic suspension dampers were reported as needing adjustment (possibly considered as a cure for the riding problems). Finally, it was mentioned that 11 defective Brown Boveri gear wheels had not yet been replaced, and that this might, in turn, lead to the scrapping of the complete axle.

After this, there appears to be little mention of further ride problems in the located files, although as will be gathered, that in no way suggests that any problems had been cured. It is more likely that there was an acceptance that the trains would always behave in that way, and the best had been achieved that was realistically possible. The concluding paragraph of the report into the test runs of 1961 commented that, "passengers who endured the Pullman were subjected to a 'tail-wagging' experience at the end of every coach".

On a lighter note, and no doubt intended to attract good publicity, an LMR press release of 28th June 1962 honoured the 100,000th passenger on the Midland Pullman. This was Mr CB Minfie of Cheadle, who was greeted when he arrived to book his usual Monday morning ticket. Arrangements were made for him to be treated as a VIP on the following Monday, 2nd July, almost exactly two years from the start of the service, and the celebrations on that day included the presentation of a commemorative silver ashtray engraved "Midland Pullman" and a special cake for Mr Minfie baked on the train. All the staff, including the Driver and "Fireman" (the old term was used by the LMR on this occasion), Guard and technicians who worked on the train, also later had their own celebratory cake. (The use of the word "technicians" in the plural is interesting, as it implies that more than one was on board the service. Was this a regular feature, or just a one off? Likewise, why is there no mention in the paperwork of the riding difficulties being reported on by these men, who were obviously skilled staff? Finally, there is no record of any correspondence between BR and the manufacturer over the riding problems. (It is somewhat ironic that the history of train sets built and running within living memory is seemingly more difficult to unravel than stock of generations past!)

For unreported reasons, there appears to have been some difficulty up to this time over the availability of spare parts, and this meant that no half-set, let alone a full-set, had been available as cover on a number of occasions during 1962. An official report of 19th September gives the exact position, and refers to the number of days that no stand-by three-car set was serviceable:

January	0
February	11
March	6
April	10
May	8
June	8
July	6
August	3
September (to 18th)	5

The service had now been running for some two years, although with only one train in operation at a time, this was the equivalent of just one year in service for each. This actually meant operational use, deducting five days for bank holidays, of some 255 days annually, representing a total available seating for the Manchester service only of 134,640 seats. (132 each way daily, x 255 for the days in service x two years). If the 100,000th passenger reported above related to the Manchester service alone, then the percentage loading was reasonable at just over 74%. However this figure should be regarded with caution as it would obviously drop if patronage on the Leicester/Nottingham service (for which figures are not known) were included.

The limited passenger numbers and revenue on the Nottingham service were clearly of concern, because in the autumn of 1963, BR announced that for a trial period beginning on 7th October, special first class single fares, reduced by an equivalent of the supplementary Pullman fare, would be available on Mondays to Fridays on journeys by the 11.15am Midland Pullman from St Pancras to Leicester, Loughborough and Nottingham. The normal fare to Nottingham of 46/6d (£2.32½) was therefore reduced to 36/6d (£1.82½) plus the 10s (50p) Pullman supplement. This was actually the second attempt to boost custom, as from 10th September 1962 the Nottingham service had been accelerated to 190 minutes from St Pancras, and had become one of the fastest schedules on BR at that time as a result.

While in public, at least, the trains appeared to be a business and financial success, their long-term future on the LMR was already being considered. A memorandum from the BTC dated 4th October 1962 sounded the first note of warning: "The trains were originally conceived as an experiment, and present difficulties then with withdrawing for periodic maintenance, as there are only a very few units, this cannot be overcome. Possibly the sets could provide information on new fittings for other vehicles in future, and also lead to other stock being upgraded to a similar standard." On this issue, it is also difficult to

A single LMR power car at an unrecorded depot. It is known that on the WR, single power cars were sometimes transferred between Old Oak Common and (presumably) Swindon, so there is reason to think that this practice was carried out on the LMR as well. (RHG Simpson)

separate the LMR operation from that of the WR, which will be discussed in the next chapter, although the reference to the "experimental" aspect was certainly new, and appears to be an excuse to cover a variety of topics; this is discussed in detail in the final chapter. Perhaps even the BTC were preparing the ground for a feared outcome even if, at that time, it was some years in the future. Certainly there is no evidence to suggest that the ordering of additional trains was ever considered. Further discussion on the sets' future, on the LMR at least, would also occur at intervals right up to 1966 and beyond.

More immediately, the subject of what do with the trains over the 1962 Christmas Holiday was under discussion, BR deciding as early as June 1962 that it intended to cancel the service between 20th December 1962 through to 2nd January 1963, and likewise on, and surrounding, the other Bank Holidays in 1963. Not surprisingly The Pullman Car Co objected to this, and cited its objections as being based on a serious loss of revenue. BR's justification for its intended action was based on figures from the equivalent period from the previous year. At this time, the loadings on the down Manchester journey from St Pancras dropped from a peak of 125 to just 40 on 22nd December 1961. The up train, though, carried its maximum compliment of 132 passengers on one occasion and over 120 on several other days. Indeed, over the 37 days surveyed, the loading was only below 100 persons on

seven occasions, with a minimum of 31. The Nottingham service, however, was very poor by comparison, with a maximum of 112 leaving St Pancras and a minimum of just six. The return was equally poor, having a maximum of 53 and a minimum of eight. While these figures represent just a sample at one period, they do support the later decision to curtail the Nottingham working. Unfortunately, from the limited data provided it is also impossible to draw valid conclusions on which days it was reasonable to expect profitability, and on which it was not. It is interesting to note that a number of journeys on the Manchester run were not day-return trips, and it would appear the Midland Pullman was used as a luxury connecting service as well as a daily means of commuting.

After 1962 and until the end of operation on the LMR, there was little of note to report. From the public's viewpoint the trains continued to operate to the usual pattern, patronage was as before and the only continuing difficulty was presumably the ride quality (although there is no correspondence on this subject after this date). Instead, activity was concentrated behind the scenes, with the LMR now working flat-out towards the electrification of the former LNWR line out of Euston, leading to the electric service being seen as the preferred one to Manchester. The continued levels of patronage on the Pullman service did pose the LMR a dilemma, however. Were they to abandon the service in favour of electrification, or continue to earn revenue from what was still a premium service, even if it was slowly becoming dated by comparison? In 1964, at least, the choice was the latter, and this is confirmed in papers lodged at Kew that state that BR would use the Pullmans even when the ex-LNWR line was electrified. It is not clear whether this meant a route change so the service operated from Euston, but in the event this detail was academic, for by the following year the decision had been reversed, and it was stated categorically that there was, "no question of using the diesel Pullman on the electrified line". However Pullman would have perhaps the last laugh, as (possibly as a direct result of the general success of the diesel Pullman service) a batch of new locomotive-hauled Pullman vehicles was built from 1962 onwards.

The period from 1962 to early 1964 passed without any known incident; indeed it has been suggested that on perhaps only three days between July 1960 and the cessation of the service were both sets out of action leading to the cancellation of the service. Further details of these failures are not reported, and it has also been suggested that a locomotive-hauled Pullman set was never used as a substitute on the Midland line. Presumably, on the rare occasions when there was no alternative, passengers were directed to an ordinary service or followed the course of action instituted after a spectacular failure on 27th February 1966.

On this occasion, the rear power car of the 6.10pm from St Pancras suffered a seized traction motor bearing, that resulted in the associated wheelset locking solid (the number of the power car involved is not known). The precise location where this occurred is not recorded, but a clue can be gleaned from the subsequent report, which states that the damaged power car was later observed at

Bedford depot. For some reason, the spare Pullman set was not available, and a replacement service with just ordinary Mark 1 coaches hauled by a Peak class diesel was used for the next two days.

Withdrawal was now only a matter of time, but there was a report that the Eastern Region had decided to take the two LMR sets to use as a separate portion of their Yorkshire Pullman, to run from Kings Cross a few minutes behind the main service, but destined for Hull. In the event, the ER was not satisfied with the riding qualities, so the proposal was abandoned; the involvement of the ER is discussed further in Chapter 7. The only other change came in March 1966, when BRB decreed that the Pullman crest be abolished, in line with the intended new corporate image. It is thought, however, that this decree was never followed with the LMR sets, which ended their days in basically the same external livery as they started.

On Friday 15th April 1966, the final departures took place from Manchester and St. Pancras, with the new electric service beginning from Euston on Monday 18th. After withdrawal, the two sets were held in store pending a decision as to their fate, although it is not known where. No doubt considerable discussion took place behind the scenes about a suitable future use, and this is discussed in the subsequent chapters. It is not believed that there was any attempt, at this time, to sell them to a foreign railway, and indeed, the sister units to the Midland Pullmans were still operating favourably on the WR at this time. With the decision to transfer both 6-car sets to the WR, they were officially withdrawn from LMR stock, and moved sometime in the late summer or autumn of 1966, it is believed to Old Oak Common, although formal transfer to WR stock would not take place until March 1967.

A final view, for the present at least, of the interior of one of the LMR vehicles. Clearly seen are the individual "call" buttons, as well as a Pullman Menu and Wine list.

(Pete Waterman/Just Like the Real Thing Collection)

COLOUR INTERLUDE

Derby North Junction in 1960, with a sparklingly clean set on the regular Manchester service. At Derby, the service was routed over the Chaddesden loop (a goods line) around the station, avoiding possible congestion there. At the time, the Midland Pullman was the only regular passenger train to use this section.   *(Colour Rail)*

Leicester London Road at 2.15pm on 5th September 1960, with the new train attracting interest from the waiting passengers. The service had arrived just five minutes earlier and was due to return to St Pancras at 2.33pm. As originally built, the LMR sets had the kitchen and pantry compartments painted all-over blue. This tended to break up the grey surrounding the rest of the windows, and was changed before the trains entered service. A similar modification was carried on the sets destined for the WR.   *(CP Boocock/Colour Rail)*

Extract from The Railway Gazette for 30th March 1960.

Left: The inside front cover of the 14-page brochure produced by Metropolitan-Cammell prior to the trains entering service. (The front cover of this brochure is reproduced on page 27.) The booklet contained a number of illustrations and drawings, including a fold-out centre section, although the only photographs were of vehicle interiors and were heavily retouched even then. Although undated, it is likely to be from the summer of 1959, at a time when the sets were almost ready, but not yet able to be fully photographed. Even so, the artistry was to a high standard, but this illustration does perhaps raise a wry smile. Notice, for example, the smiling driver (the train is single-manned), the deliberately unclear name on the side of the power unit (is it a 6-car Birmingham Pullman?) and the lack of continuity of the white paint along the length of the kitchen car (this is discussed within the text).

A **FIRST CLASS** ACHIEVEMENT

Right: As referred to in the text, at the time of their introduction, the new trains seemed very much to capture the imagination of the period, resulting in them featuring in several brochures and advertisements. This is the cover of a 1960 brochure produced by J Stone & Co, who were responsible for several items including the inter-coach electrical couplings, the alternator on the auxiliary engines and the air-conditioning equipment.

Equipment for
BRITISH RAILWAYS NEW DIESEL PULLMAN TRAINS

AUXILIARY POWER · AIR-CONDITIONING · HEATING · LIGHTING · ETC.

Platforms 5 and 6 at Paddington on 12th September 1960, just after 9.35am. The inaugural service from Bristol (left) stands alongside the first public arrival from Birmingham, the coincident arrivals being intentionally stage-managed by the WR for the occasion (see Chapter 6). Vehicle numbers were unfortunately not recorded, but the sideways view of the Bristol crew's white coat uniforms can be seen within the drivers' cab. (Michael Farr/Colour Rail)

Swindon Works on an unknown date, and with an unidentified power car in view. In the foreground is believed to be the main MAN engine and generator from one of the power cars, while the blanks normally covering the headlamp lights also show up well in the photograph. (Although not known for certain, the blanks and the transparent red disc were probably stored inside the cab.)

(HJ Ashman/ Adrian Vaughan Collection)

(Ian Shawyer Collection)

Much discussion has taken place in recent years over the interior colours of the sets, and this subject is discussed in detail in Chapter 4. Here is a press view entitled "First class saloon showing seat adjustment control". The illustration comes from an official BR(WR) booklet of 1960 intended to introduce the public to the "Pullman Diesel Express Services". The colour schemes in the vehicles have been mentioned elsewhere, but this is an appropriate place to refer to the variations that existed in first class. Scheme 1: passenger saloon walls – French grey Lanide; passenger saloon partitions and doors – Rio rosewood veneer; carpet - "Cortina Kingfisher" (irregular blue trace on a black background); seats - narrow vertical red and Navy blue stripes; seat backs and arm pads - grey Lanide; arm sides and pedestals - black Lanide. Scheme 2: similar to scheme 1, but with passenger saloon partitions and doors finished with Macassar ebony veneer; carpet in "Cortina Cardinal" (irregular red trace on black background) and seating colours changed to blue with Navy blue vertical stripes. The coach partitions were inlaid to a depth of one eighth of an inch using small pieces of plastic, wood, marble and metal. The whole was then covered with a transparent resin, sanded and polished to give a sparkling appearance. Also of note is the surround on the inside of the window, gold in first class and aluminium in second. Over the years, there were a number of variations in the size and style of the antimacassars used. (David Hyde Collection)

On the Midland main line, a superbly clean LMR 6-car set passes Wigston South Signal Box in June 1963.
(B Metcalfe/Colour Rail)

At speed near Hathern, south of Kegworth, on 13th May 1965. Note the parking of the wiper on the second-man's side, a problem that was supposed to have been overcome by this time. The drab appearance of the vehicle sides indicates that daily cleaning of the exteriors no longer took place at this time.
(Colour Rail)

At speed near Acocks Green in 1962. *(Michael Mensing)*

Ready for departure from Paddington, believed to be very early in the life of the sets.
(Colour Rail)

4.40pm at Paddington on 3rd August 1961, with the two sets displaying obvious variations in head-lamp codes. Notice the use of platforms 5 and 6 again; these appear to have been the regular haunts of the trains. It is likely that the set on the left (on platform 6) will shortly be leaving as the 4.50pm service to Birmingham and Wolverhampton, with intermediate stops at Leamington Spa General and Solihull. That on the right is probably due to form the 4.55pm South Wales Pullman to Swansea, with stops at Newport, Cardiff General, Bridgend, and Port Talbot. It appears that this train is being prepared for service.
(Peter Brumby)

Under the wires, between Coventry and Birmingham in 1966 - the final days of the Pullman service from Paddington. The fact that the train is operating over the former LNWR route raises a number of questions. Did the last days of the Birmingham service see all services running this way, or was this simply due to engineering work? The destination blind implies that it was a normal service, although the train identification number, 1Z66, displayed inside the windscreen tends to contradict this. (Michael Mensing)

The down Birmingham Pullman racing from Whitehouse Farm Tunnel, north of Beaconsfield on 9th August 1962.

(John Bell)

Photographs of the trains at Wolverhampton are rare, so it was particularly pleasing to locate this view of a trial at Wolverhampton Low Level in August 1960. Again, the set attracts a considerable amount of interest, with its striking livery contrasting well with a somewhat drab location.
(J Clarke/ Colour Rail)

The Paddington area in 1961 or 1962. The headcode lights are a little confusing; the left one appears white, but the strong red centre light implies that the set is leaving, and it might even be an empty stock working to Old Oak Common.
(HJ Ashman/Adrian Vaughan Collection)

This superb Michael Mensing image shows an early morning service near Widley Manor. The train is the 7.00am from Wolverhampton, and has just restarted following the Solihull stop on 9th May 1963. Of note is the indicator blind on the side of the Guard's compartment; this was only fitted to the WR sets. The once pristine blue livery has weathered somewhat, particularly below floor level, where the underframe and bogies have taken on a decidedly brown tone.

(Michael Mensing)

The Birmingham suburbs - a WR set near Bentley Heath in 1963.

(Michael Mensing)

The old and the new between Moreton Cutting and Didcot in May 1965. The Didcot East Junction splitting distant semaphore signals are seen in their final days, with the new MAS posts erected, but covered with an "X". The train is an up service from Bristol or Swansea.

(Ron Price/Adrian Vaughan Collection)

Sonning Power Station, east of Reading, with the train about to enter the famous cutting of the same name. The 8.15am service from Bristol Temple Meads is seen in October 1965. (HJ Ashman/Adrian Vaughan Collection)

The transitional livery (Nanking blue with yellow ends) on a down service in Sonning Cutting. Unfortunately, no information is available about the date, but it is likely to have been around 1966 or 1967.

(HJ Ashman/Adrian Vaughan Collection)

The final years of the Pullman - storming out of Paddington in 1970.   *(HJ Ashman/Adrian Vaughan Collection)*

Previous page top: The heyday of the Blue Pullman, and the premier Western Region service. The afternoon Birmingham and Wolverhampton departure from Paddington is seen at Solihull in the summer of 1962.   (Michael Mensing)

Previous page bottom: Despite being destined never to work to Bournemouth on a regular service, some specials did operate on the Southern Region (see also the black and white photograph on page 132). This is Bromley South with a former WR 8-car set photographed on 15th July 1972; the train is in good clean external condition. Although unusual, this working was nothing compared to what must be the most unlikely excursion planned for one of the sets around 1966, following the withdrawal of the 6-car units from the LMR. The suggestion was that a group from Bristol would charter a train to run to, of all places, Paris! The logistics of the exercise for the time are mind-blowing, and it is perhaps not surprising that nothing came of the idea.   (Southern Electric Group)

Chapter 6

IN SERVICE ON THE WESTERN REGION

It might seem that the early years of the Pullman services on the Western Region were overshadowed by the publicity surrounding those operating out of St. Pancras. The WR had three sets instead of the LMR's two, and the WR sets were made up of eight cars carrying both first- and second-class Pullman accommodation (108 first and 120 second), so there was more risk of difficulties developing with the WR sets. However, those difficulties never gained the same media attention as those that affected the sets operating on the Midland route. It might just be that news quickly becomes stale, and while the LMR might have been the first to attract praise for operating the new trains, they also became the first to attract criticism. Perhaps someone at Paddington was content to sit back and recall the story of the tortoise and the hare!

Testing, familiarisation and training of the new units on the WR took place from the start of 1960, and as confidence grew, trials began over the routes that would later be used, in addition to visits to more lightly-used lines, in particular the one from Bristol to Birmingham via Barnt Green. (Testing, running-in and familiarisation trials over lightly-used routes was nothing new; an example a

few years earlier was when Swindon used sections of the former Midland & South Western Junction Railway line to test DMU units built at the Wiltshire works.) In addition to this type of running, there were return visits to the manufacturers at Birmingham and to the works at Swindon for necessary modifications and adjustments. The report by AE Robson of Euston in November 1959 (see page 26) refers to difficulties encountered during the trial running of the LMR sets, but no similar report has been located on the early WR trials. No doubt an exchange of information between the regions took place anyway, with some modifications being made to the WR sets before they were delivered.

Such activities occupied the spring and early summer of 1960, and it was reported by Paddington that the WR sets were ready to begin operations in July 1960, possibly even at the same time as the LMR sets. However, before this date was announced to the public, it was postponed for two months by Paddington, resulting in some sharp questioning from BRB. In reply, Paddington were nothing but honest, citing the considerable difficulty in finding men willing to transfer to the new trains, or even

Pre-service trial run on 26th April 1960, passing through Banbury probably destined for Birmingham or Wolverhampton. To the right, the group of WRAC members are seemingly in the process of boarding the service to Woodford Halse. Services from Banbury over this connection to the former Great Central route ceased in September 1966.

(Kidderminster Railway Museum Collection)

finding new catering staff to recruit. Eventually, they requested permission to recruit from outside (implying that there was an embargo on recruitment at the time). There appears to have been far less union resistance over the manning of the WR sets, and it could be that potential staff would not take up the new roles for fear of becoming embroiled in an ongoing labour dispute. BRB, however, could pontificate in safety, and it appears from correspondence that some pressure was exerted to find men as quickly as possible.

Eventually, the new service was advertised to its potential clientele in August 1960, but somehow, the impact was not quite as striking as when the new trains had begun on the LMR, and indeed, the brochures and other paperwork generated by the WR were somewhat bland by comparison.

Public running began from Monday 12th September 1960, although preparation for the new workings had not

just involved crew training, as new "shore" facilities had to be installed at Paddington, Old Oak Common, Bristol Temple Meads, Dr Day's Sidings – Bristol, and Cannock Road Sidings – Wolverhampton. (It is not clear whether a shore supply was installed at Swansea when the workings were later extended there, but the likelihood is that it was.)

Two sets were required for the WR operation, both running in the up direction in the mornings, one from Bristol and the other from Wolverhampton. The up departure from Temple Meads left at 7.45pm, and ran non-stop to Paddington via the Badminton line, arriving at 9.35am. This was a 110-minute timing, which was quickly seized on by pundits as being five minutes slower than the contemporary diesel-hauled Bristolian service over the same route, on which no supplement was charged. The up morning service from Wolverhampton departed from the Low Level station at 7.00am, and called at Birmingham Snow Hill, Solihull and Leamington Spa General, with the

Pre-service test and training run in the Birmingham suburbs, passing Acock's Green and South Yardley station. The train was recorded late in the day of 16th August 1961, and so might be emulating what was to be the afternoon service from Paddington. All three men in the cab are wearing their white uniforms, complete with caps, although it would seem that even from an early stage, some men chose their own attire whenever possible. (Michael Mensing)

Arrival at Solihull on the first day of working, 12th September 1960. Unfortunately, loadings for the first day are not available, but it was certainly not full all the way, as is shown by the empty seats in the leading power car seen in the next picture. *(Michael Mensing)*

Departure from Solihull, with W60094 leading, at 6.37pm, also on the first day of working, 12th September 1960. The train was no doubt given a clear road for the occasion. The two youthful spotters are in the prescribed boys' uniform of the period – short trousers! *(Michael Mensing)*

*3.10pm at platforms 7 and 6 at Paddington on 27th October 1960. The two sets will probably form the 4.50pm to Bir-
mingham and the 4.55pm to Bristol, although it must be said that their arrival at the platforms at this time does seem
somewhat premature; the set on the left displays the standard headcode for empty coaching stock. Note the presence of
the white-coated crew in the cab of the train on platform 6; this uniform is visible in several contemporary WR views.
The photograph also appears to confirm that a shore-supply was available at platforms 7 and 8, and not just at platforms
5 and 6. It is believed that the DMU occupying platform 5 (displaying 2A58) would shortly leave on the 3.15pm service
to Windsor. Only one steam engine is visible, a 97xx series condensing pannier tank, the number of which cannot be
made out. Finally, notice the line-up of contemporary cars, the majority still being of British manufacture at this time.*

(Ian Shawyer Collection)

same scheduled arrival time of 9.35am.

On the first day of working, a special effort was
made by the operating department to ensure that, from Old
Oak Common onwards, both trains would converge simultaneously on parallel tracks so that they would run side by
side for the final leg into Paddington. In order to achieve
this, a signalling inspector was present in Old Oak Common signal box, and no doubt a special effort was made to
ensure there were no hold-ups en-route. Even so, it was
inevitable that one train would arrive slightly before the
other, and it is believed that the one from Wolverhampton
did so (although another source refers to the Bristol service as being the first to arrive!) However, both trains arrived near enough together to run side-by-side as intended
for the final three miles, much to the delight of the waiting
photographers, Press and public alike, who were there to
record the scene.

Michael Farr, a regular traveller on the morning up
service from Bristol, recounts that for the first day, and for
several days subsequently, there was a general euphoria
amongst the passengers over what they all perceived to be
something rather special. Initially, the passenger compliment was often accompanied by reporters and photographers, and Michael recalls that the ride was not particularly smooth even when the sets were brand new, as reported in the previous chapter.

He recalls that within a very few days, small absor-
bent paper coasters were introduced between the cup and
saucer whenever a drink was served by a steward. These
achieved two results; firstly the rattle of crockery was reduced, and secondly, slops of liquid from the cup were less
noticeable. (See also "With a Splash" on page 75).

Both sets had a midday "fill-in" turn, the morning
up service from Wolverhampton returning after only 30
minutes in London as the 10.05am down to Bristol. Departure from Bristol, after another very short turnaround,
was at 12.30pm, although this time it was routed via Bath,
arriving at Paddington at 2.25pm. Here, servicing, cleaning and restocking took place, with the final departure of
the day at 4.55pm for Bristol non-stop via Badminton. The

The down mid-day Pullman (12.10pm from Paddington) recorded entering Snow Hill on 28th March 1961. The news-stand is operated by Messrs Wymans, who were once a familiar sight at numerous stations. On the left, the tail end of an up freight is disappearing into the tunnel. (Michael Mensing)

fill-in turn for the morning up Bristol set was the 12.10pm Paddington to Birmingham Snow Hill and return, calling at Leamington only; the 84 minutes allowed between Leamington and Paddington was the fastest ever schedule between these points. For this set, servicing, cleaning and restocking was presumably accomplished during the morning at Paddington. Official BR records of the period refer to each of the sets covering around 480 miles daily.

These arrangements only remained in place for a few weeks, as from 17th October, the morning and evening runs of the Bristol train were rerouted in order to call at Bath Spa. This was as a result of complaints from passengers wishing to travel from Paddington to Bath Spa, as they had seen their own regular fast service retimed to accommodate the new service. It is believed that this change added a further five minutes to the schedule in both directions.

1960 concluded with the incident of 5th December, referred to briefly in the previous chapter. The train affected was the 10.05am from Paddington, which was immediately taken out of service at Swindon with the passengers continuing their journeys on the steam-hauled Merchant Venturer. The afternoon return from Bristol was covered by Castle class 5056 "Earl of Powis" and a 10-coach set, although further details of the vehicles used are not known. For the evening working, the spare Pullman set was used, and remained in use for several days.

The derailment of an unrelated train near Swindon

on 10th February 1961 saw the up service from Bristol diverted via Devizes - believed to have been the first time one of the sets worked over this route.

Apart from the obvious differences in formation between the trains running on the WR and the LMR, a further external difference was the provision of a route indicator blind located in the Guard's compartment of the power cars, that could be set to read either "Bristol Pullman" or "Birmingham Pullman", due to the fact that the units could be used on either of the two routes. Similarly, the carriage sides were simply lettered "Pullman", without specifying Bristol, Birmingham or Wolverhampton.

Staff uniforms were identical for the catering staff, but the WR drivers were issued with white knee-length overcoats and matching white hats, that quickly led to them being given nicknames of "ice-cream sellers" or "milkmen", together with associated ribald comments. Such clothing was considered as trivialising the impact of the new trains, and in contrast, the LMR drivers wore smart dark green "battledress fatigues". Despite the comments, some WR crews wore the white uniform as late as 1963, and some might even have survived beyond that date. A travelling fitter was also provided, who would occupy the unused Guard's compartment in one of the power cars.

Looking back over 40 years later, two measures were taken at the time that nowadays might cause a wry smile. The first is that in the public timetable, great prominence was given to the trains, with a single page in

99

Above: The Birmingham Pullman in the London outskirts between Kensal Green and Old Oak Common. Nearby, is the Hammersmith Hospital and Wormwood Scrubs prison, from where the spy, George Blake, escaped in October 1966.
Opposite page: In service on the Western Region. The down Bristol Pullman service emerging into daylight from the 262-yard Twerton Long Tunnel west of Bath on 29th August 1961. *(Ivo Peters Collection)*

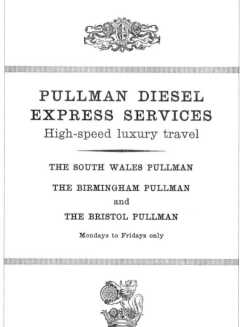

PULLMAN DIESEL EXPRESS SERVICES
High-speed luxury travel

THE SOUTH WALES PULLMAN

THE BIRMINGHAM PULLMAN
and
THE BRISTOL PULLMAN

Mondays to Fridays only

By comparison with the LMR, surviving publicity from the WR has been hard to locate. Indeed what handbills have been found appear bland and in some respects unimaginative. Two examples are shown here: on the left is a simple sheet without illustrations dating from September 1961, which apart from the train times also explained, "From time to time it will be necessary to take each of the trains out of service for a period and this will be done by utilising a traditional Pullman train hauled by either a Diesel or Steam locomotive but the seating will be identical". The leaflet displays a remarkable similarity to that shown on Page 32. The publicity material on the right is from September 1964.

(Antony M Ford Collection)

101

PASSENGER TRAIN ALTERATIONS

Improved luxury Pullman facilities of special interest to passengers travelling between **PADDINGTON, BATH and BRISTOL**

Commencing **Monday, 17th October, 1960**, and continuing experimentally Mondays to Fridays until further notice the undermentioned Pullman Diesel Express Services will call **additionally** at Bath Spa:

7.45 am (PULLMAN) BRISTOL (T. M.) to PADDINGTON
will start at 7.40 am, arrive Bath Spa 7.55 am, depart 7.57 am and arrive Paddington 9.35 am.

4.55 pm (PULLMAN) PADDINGTON to BRISTOL (T. M.)
will arrive Bath Spa 6.32 pm, depart 6.34 pm and arrive Bristol (Temple Meads) 6.50 pm.

In order to provide this improved facility the following alterations will also operate:

7.0 am WESTON-SUPER-MARE GENERAL to PADDINGTON
will depart Bristol (Temple Meads) 7.45 am, Bath Spa 8.5 am (arrive 8.2 am), Chippenham 8.26 am (arrive 8.24 am), Didcot 9.9 am (arrive 9.7 am) and arrive Paddington 10.7 am.

4.15 pm PADDINGTON to PLYMOUTH
will start at 4.5 pm and depart Reading General 4.47 pm (arrive 4.43 pm), Swindon 5.37 pm (arrive 5.34 pm), Chippenham 5.59 pm (arrive 5.55 pm), Bath Spa 6.21 pm (arrive 6.17 pm) and arrive Bristol (Temple Meads) 6.40 pm, depart 7.0 pm, and on as shown in Time Table.

Whilst these alterations are experimental and may be subject to adjustment at a later date, they are designed to improve the position for the majority of our regular patrons.

Paddington Station, London, W.2

J. R. HAMMOND, General Manager

Published by British Railways (Western Region) BR.35004 Printed by Harrison & Sons, Ltd., St. Martin's Lane, London, W.C.2 8848

Embarrassment for the authorities in the autumn of 1960. Here is confirmation of the timetable changes brought about by pressure from commuters in Bath. The original notice was printed in red and blue.

(Ian Shawyer Collection)

the coloured introduction section devoted to each of the new services. In the working timetable, however, the need to spell out the basics of fixed formation working was still considered necessary, and for some years the symbols ♠ ♠ appeared, meaning, "Four wheeled vehicles must NOT be conveyed on this train". The thought of a shunter attaching a cattle truck to the rear of a Pullman set, let alone said vehicle bouncing along at 90mph, is perhaps best left to the imagination!

The same public timetable also included a note that "Dogs, motors/scooters, perambulators, etc are not conveyed on this service". Again some of these may seem obvious, not least due to space constraints, but in the first days of operation, it was quite acceptable to arrive at Paddington (or Bristol or Birmingham) with "Pongo", and he would be carried accordingly. To begin with, this was probably within the passenger compartment, but this

quickly changed to dogs being accommodated in the front Guard's compartment.

This was the case, one day, when two German Shepherd dogs belonging to one of the passengers were secured in what was a rather noisy area. The travelling fitter, needing to gain access to the front engine compartment, was prevented from doing so by the two dogs, panic-stricken by being confronted with the roar from the 1,000hp MAN engine just a few feet away. Not surprisingly, all dogs were barred shortly afterwards.

On another occasion, a Bristol-bound set suffered a defect so severe that the crew was wary about stopping to gain assistance for fear of being unable to start again. Somehow this was communicated to the operating staff along the route (the traditional note on a piece of paper attached to a lump of coal, and lobbed out near a signalbox, was clearly inappropriate) with the result that the train was diverted through the platform lines at Swindon, and a door held open for a fitter to join the rear of the unit without it stopping. This was successfully accomplished, but although it was necessary for the fitter to walk through the train, he was prevented from doing so by the Conductor, unless and until, he covered the top of his overalls with a jacket. (It is not known why the travelling fitter could not fix the problem, so it is possible that the man picked up at Swindon was carrying a necessary spare part.)

There was an amusing sequel to the incident of the dogs, which occurred in the bad winter of 1962/3. It appears that HRH Princess Margaret, together with Lord Snowdon and their entourage (including two Sealyham dogs) were stranded at Birmingham, unable to return to London by air due to the prevailing weather. Accordingly, a rapid change of plan resulted in the party finding their way to Snow Hill where space was to be found for them on the Pullman service. This change had been notified to Paddington, but there was a fear that the conductor on the service (who was known to be something of a martinet) would very likely refuse the Royal party access purely due to the presence of the dogs. Paddington therefore spent some considerable effort attempting to raise Snow Hill, and in particular the Station Master or Senior Inspector, to advise them of the predicament. At the time, Paddington were already extremely busy due to the numerous delays resulting from the weather, and a lot of other services were delayed even more than might have been, simply because of the time spent ensuring all would go smoothly with the Royal party. The final twist is that, regardless of their intentions, the control office staff were later criticised over the time spent and the additional delays elsewhere. There is no record as to where the dogs travelled on that particular day; perhaps "in comfort" would be a fitting tailpiece.

It has been suggested that at least one other individual was afforded a similar VIP service, this time on a London-bound service from Cardiff for the benefit of the singer, Shirley Bassey. A power car was set aside for the sole use of Welsh singer, together with her own travelling

PULLMAN

The subject of the WR crew uniforms has been mentioned within the text and is indeed one of the areas much discussed amongst Pullman devotees. Whilst no doubt well intentioned, they were hardly a tailored fit. Possibly some of the ribald comments came from other men secretly jealous of the prestige associated with the Pullman workings, although continued leg-pulling did eventually make some crews discard the dust coat for more conventional attire. The decal and wording read "Western Region" and "Pullman".

Above left: An unidentified crew at Paddington on 17ᵗʰ May 1961, who had just brought the up Pullman from Bristol. Both were recorded as "senior drivers", and Inspector Whitley is standing behind them. Ivo Peters had accompanied the crew in the cab of the train from Bath on that occasion.

(Ivo Peters Collection)

Above right: Another un-named crew, possibly at Swansea.
(Antony M Ford Collection)

Right: Proof that some men continued to wear their original issue white uniform. Driver Fred Forster of Bristol is seen shaking hands with George Johnson, the Pullman conductor at Bristol in late 1962, on the occasion of Driver Forster's retirement after 48 years service.

(BR Western Region Magazine)

BRISTOL PULLMAN

The down Pullman, running non-stop through what is now platform 4 at Reading General, passing an SR 2-BIL unit. The electric is standing at the platforms at the east end of Reading station that were added after the closure of the ex-Southern Railway station. A permanent speed limit applied through platform 4, which gave passengers the impression that the trains were deliberately varying speed en-route, so as to present a fast-slow-fast-slow image - a feature that was commented on by OS Nock in the Railway Magazine. However, he was of the opinion that, apart from locations where necessary slowing occurred, such as Reading, it was caused by easy scheduling and general line congestion. (Could it be that drivers and conductors co-operated at the times when it was necessary to serve the soup!)

(Ian Shawyer Collection)

Opposite page, top: A down service has just left Paddington and is passing Royal Oak. To the right is one of the early series North British Warship diesels, complete with a contemporary headboard of the period.

(Antony M Ford Collection)

Opposite page, bottom: The down Bristol Pullman approaching West Ealing, believed to be sometime in 1963. The WR power cars accommodated just second-class Pullman passengers, the following formation being a second-class parlour car, first-class kitchen car, and first-class parlour car, with the remaining four cars of the 8-car set being the same, but in reverse order. First-class accommodation was identified externally by the figure 1 on the doors, but there was never a need for a numeral on the LMR sets, as these were all first class; "2+1" seating was installed in both classes. On the WR, the kitchen car was the opposite way round to that on the LMR sets.

(PJ Lynch)

First and second class Pullman supplement tickets for the Bristol route (from 1964, 1964, and 1962 respectively). Second class Pullman was identified by being produced on pink card, the shade of which varied slightly over time.

(Antony M Ford and Michael Farr Collections)

Table 7

THE
SOUTH WALES PULLMAN
(LIMITED ACCOMMODATION)

LONDON, NEWPORT, CARDIFF, BRIDGEND, PORT TALBOT and SWANSEA

WEEK DAYS
(Mondays to Fridays)

	am			pm
Swansea (High Street) .. ..dep	6 40	London (Paddington) .. ..dep	4 55
Port Talbot (General) .. .. „	7 3	Newport .. ..arr	7 2
Bridgend .. .. „	7 19	Cardiff (General) .. .. .. „	7 20
Cardiff (General) .. .. .. „	7 50	Bridgend .. .. „	7 49
Newport .. .. „	8 8	Port Talbot (General) .. .. „	8 8
London (Paddington) .. ..arr	10 15	Swansea (High Street) .. .. „	8 40

MEALS AND REFRESHMENTS SERVED AT EVERY SEAT
Supplementary Charges (for each single journey)

Between	LONDON (Paddington)		NEWPORT		CARDIFF		BRIDGEND		PORT TALBOT		SWANSEA	
	1st	2nd	1st	2nd	1st	2nd	1st	2nd	1st	2nd	1st	2nd
NEWPORT	7/-	4/-	–	–	1/-	1/-	2/-	1/-	3/-	1/6	3/-	1/6
CARDIFF (General)	8/-	4/6	1/-	1/-	–	–	2/-	1/-	2/-	1/-	2/-	1/-
BRIDGEND	8/-	4/6	2/-	1/-	2/-	1/-	–	–	1/-	1/-	2/-	1/-
PORT TALBOT (General)	10/-	5/-	3/-	1/6	2/-	1/-	1/-	1/-	–	–	1/-	1/-
SWANSEA (High Street)	10/-	5/-	3/-	1/6	2/-	1/-	2/-	1/-	1/-	1/-	–	–

The Supplementary Charge is payable in addition to the usual First or Second Class Fare applicable to the journey being made.

THE NUMBER OF PASSENGERS CARRIED IS LIMITED TO THE SEATING ACCOMMODATION AVAILABLE.

Dogs, motor/scooters, perambulators, etc. not conveyed on this service.

Seats can be reserved in advance at stations and usual agencies for journeys from and to all the stations shewn above. Subsequent reservations may be effected with the Pullman Car Conductor on the train if accommodation is available.

Pullman Car Tickets will only be issued subject to these conditions.

For many years the public timetables contained a section of coloured pages, giving details of the premier services, which were repeated again within the main body of the timetable. As might be expected, a page was devoted to each of the Pullman services, this example showing the Birmingham working. The note about dogs not being carried should be noted. Children's fares were only available on the South Wales Pullman, other than that there were no discounts.

canine companions.

With three sets available on the WR, one was kept as a spare, normally in the new purpose-built 3-road Pullman shed erected at Old Oak Common between the former steam shed and the carriage sidings. (Incidentally, decades later and currently used by one of the privatised rail infrastructure maintenance companies, this is still referred to as "The Pullman Shed".)

Utilisation up to the summer of 1961 meant that two of the three 8-car sets were in use, and allowing for the spare set, this meant that each train was in service for ten days out of 21. Loading figures from BR sources for the WR trains in the early days are not known, although the *Daily Telegraph* article of October 1960 that quoted the Midland Pullman as running at less than 60% capacity, quoted 70% for the Bristol service and 90% for the Bir-

mingham service. (Doubtless, the traffic originating at, or continuing on to, Wolverhampton was considerably less.)

Despite the lack of any definitive information from the first days of the service, some maintenance difficulties were reported on 20th September 1962, but these mainly concerned the availability of spare parts. It would seem that the LMR and WR assisted each other with spares when necessary, although official information about the number of spares held, as well as difficulties obtaining specific items, is contradictory in the surviving paperwork.

Presumably, the WR worked to similar maintenance and inspection schedules as their colleagues on the LMR, although maintenance was likely to have taken slightly longer, simply because of the additional two cars; again maintenance was scheduled for weekends. Despite having 50% spare capacity, it appears that on the WR, at least, there were times when both the main sets and the stand-by set were unavailable, possibly due to the spare set being stabled "out of position", to cover a breakdown.

However, regardless of the reliability or otherwise of the trains, Paddington apparently had far more confidence in the sets, with the result that an expansion of the diesel Pullman operation was scheduled for the start of the autumn timetable in 1961. This took the form of a modern diesel replacement for the steam-hauled South Wales Pullman commencing on 11th September 1961 (although another report refers to the Swansea service beginning from 31st August). The diesel South Wales Pullman service operated on weekdays between Swansea and Paddington, and called at major stations each way between Swansea and Cardiff, then non-stop from Cardiff to Paddington. It was a commercial success from the outset, but it did mean there was now no longer a spare diesel set if it were needed. At the same time, the steam-hauled service was withdrawn, although its stock was retained as a potential loco-hauled stand-by train set. This rake is likely to have been based at Old Oak Common, and in its earliest form, included two BR standard Mark 1 open firsts.

Despite the fact that the WR was still forming its other named trains in traditional chocolate and cream livery, the authorities were very anxious that the two Mark 1s should exactly match the rest of the train. Accordingly, a supply of authentic Pullman umber and cream was despatched to Swindon, but the result was anything but satisfactory, with no attempt being made to apply any type of lining whatsoever — not even to emulate that on a conventional BR vehicle, let alone the more elaborate Pullman style. At a later stage, the spare train set was re-formed with traditional Pullman vehicles only, and with the suggestion that they should be named after rivers. Among the names selected were "Wye", "Severn", "Thames" and "Avon".

According to RW Kidner in *Pullman Trains in Britain*, the formation of the spare set was originally numbers 27, 249, 169 and 54 plus "Cecelia", together with first opens, W3093 and W3094. This formation is known to have altered at various times, such as on 26th August 1964, when three second-class Eastern Region cars (340, 352 and 344) were used as stand-in first-class accommodation

An undated view of a set at Paddington. From the station clock, part of which is just visible on the extreme left, the time would appear to be around 10.40 am, meaning that this could be stock that had arrived as the morning up service from either Bristol or Swansea.

on the 1.00pm service from Birmingham. The reason for this was officially stated to be that the available seating more closely matched that of the 8-car WR Pullman sets (further information is given in Appendix A).

Whenever a spare set was in use, the catering staff nicknamed it the "Wells-Fargo" set. This was an unkind reference to the contemporary "Western" television series that featured a locomotive and a rake of elderly Pullman cars, to which the spare set was perceived to bear a striking resemblance.

If one of the stand-by sets was in use, it was not unusual for some passengers to object to paying the Pullman supplement due to old fashioned stock being used, and the policy in such cases was that they would be refunded without question. One passenger allegedly complained when seeing his mother off at Paddington on a stand-by set, "I am paying extra for her to travel, just to watch a man walk up and down the coach in a white suit."

As mentioned in the previous chapter, by 1962, the LMR also had a spare set of locomotive-hauled Pullman vehicles at its disposal, courtesy of the Southern Region. The first use of these vehicles was both unforeseen and, to say the least, difficult. Charles Long recounts a story in relation to the Birmingham Pullman shortly after the WR West Midland lines were transferred to the LMR:

"Some fault had been discovered during the rou-

tine weekend examination of the rostered diesel unit. The seating layouts and numbering in the older-style Pullmans, compared with the diesel cars, was totally different. Carefully prepared, equivalent seating diagrams to match a 5-car rake to the 6-car, first-class Midland Pullman were useless when it came to substituting for the 8-car first- and second-class Birmingham train. Having seen the stand-in set for the first time only a short while beforehand, the Conductor had quite a job sorting out his customers on the well-filled Monday morning journey to Paddington. Confusion was confounded en-route, as regular passengers, expecting their normal diesel unit, waited in their usual places at intermediate calling points, first-class towards the centre, second-class at each end. Since the "genuine" first-class locomotive-hauled cars included both brake-ends, many second-class ticket-holders found themselves enjoying unexpected armchair luxury, while certain first-class passengers were somewhat less-lavishly accommodated in the sometime seconds."

The increase from 66.6% utilisation of the three sets achieved by the WR from this time was in stark contrast to the continuing 50% utilisation of two sets on the LMR, raising a number of questions, the first and most obvious being why, if the WR could have all its sets ready for use, did the LMR feel unable to do so? Did the pro-

The 4.50pm Paddington to Wolverhampton (Low Level) arriving at platform 4 of Birmingham Snow Hill on 5th April 1962. Assuming the service to be on time, it should be just before 6.55pm, which was the scheduled departure for the last leg of the journey. Notice, in particular, the "Pullman Car H" sign. These signs were provided to help passengers locate where a particular car would come to rest when the train arrived; similar signs were provided for the other vehicles in the train. To the extreme right is D1002 "Western Explorer", one of the brand new Western class diesels, which was less than three weeks old when photographed. This particular machine was present, together with a few other publicity-related vehicles and items, for "Western Railway Week". *(Michael Mensing)*

Opposite page, top: The up lunchtime (1.00pm) service from Birmingham running through Harbury cutting south east of Leamington Spa on 27th September 1965. This was the schedule operated by the "Wells-Fargo" set, at the time it was involved in the accident at Knowle and Dorridge in August 1963. *(Michael Mensing)*

Opposite page, bottom: Included to show the white buffers painted on at least one WR power car (which one, and why, are not recorded), this is the 4.50pm down service from Paddington passing over Lapworth water troughs north of Leamington Spa on 31st May 1966. It could be that the painting had been done for a previous special working, but because it was unlikely that any vehicles would ever be coupled to the front of the power car, the effect would have lasted for some considerable time. *(Michael Mensing)*

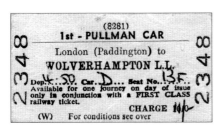

First and second class Pullman supplement tickets for the Birmingham route, all of which date from 1964. *(Antony M Ford Collection)*

An unidentified power car at Swindon for repair or overhaul. As with the LMR sets, it is believed the WR units were over-hauled as necessary on their home region, and there is no evidence to suggest that recourse was made to the manufactur-ers after initial delivery.   *(R. Blencowe)*

posed LMR Liverpool service stem from the observation of the 100% utilisation being achieved by its neighbour? Likewise, was maintenance an issue, preventing one of the regions operating at full capacity.

Unfortunately though, only odd examples of fail-ures on the WR are recorded, one being in September 1962, when Hymek D7023 was observed with a locomo-tive-hauled Pullman set deputising for the up South Wales set. Another was when D1006 "Western Stalwart" was in charge of locomotive-hauled stock on the Birmingham service (whether morning or midday is not reported).

The most dramatic replacement, however, was on Thursday 15th August 1963, when the loco-hauled Pull-man set replacing the lunchtime up Birmingham Pullman, hauled by D1040 "Western Queen", collided with a goods train being shunted at Knowle and Dorridge. The crew reported they had been travelling at 80mph just before the accident, and on sighting adverse signals, managed to bring the speed down to 20mph at the point of collision. Fortunately, there were no serious injuries, and the strongly built rolling stock from 1923 stood up well, with the train remaining upright and intact. The subsequent enquiry absolved the train crew, and focussed blame on the signalman. Some comments were made about the braking characteristics of the train, which despite the age of the rolling stock, implied that it was better than that on the diesel Pullman.

Interestingly, *Modern Railways* recorded that when recourse had to be made to the loco-hauled, stand-by Pull-man set, loadings were not adversely affected. Passen-gers, of course, would be unlikely to be aware that the usual diesel set was unavailable, so continuous use of the standby set over a protracted period might well have had a different effect on the loadings. It was stated in the same magazine that up to late 1964 the three diesel sets operat-ing on the WR had failed in service on a total of 19 occa-sions since 1960.

Possibly the worst day on the WR was 11th April 1963, when for various reasons, all three sets were out of action. On that day, the Birmingham service was in charge of D1006 "Western Stalwart", the Bristol service, D834 "Pathfinder", and the South Wales service, Hymek number D7066. Rolling stock details were not recorded, but presumably use was made of both the WR and LMR loco-hauled rakes; there is certainly no evidence that a diesel Pullman set was ever the subject of an inter-regional loan.

An unusual means of publicising the sets took place in 1963, when public announcements were made referring to the impending withdrawal for overhaul of some of the sets. The cleverly worded announcements ensured that the trains remained in the forefront of the minds of the clientele they carried:

"After intensive service since their introduction in

On 22nd February 1962, the Chairman of the British Railways Board, Dr Richard Beeching, together with the General Manager of the Western Region, Mr Stanley Raymond, made a well-publicised cab ride in the South Wales Pullman between Paddington and Cardiff. Swansea drivers, Frederick Day and William Lewis, were in charge of the train, and the group is seen here seen in the cab of the train at Paddington. It seems that an extra seat was fitted for Mr Raymond – a case of RHIP (Rank hath its privileges)! The train was met by a considerable Press throng at Cardiff, as the VIP visit was intended to establish the future shape of the railways in the South Wales Valleys. Sadly the results of that visit are now well known, of course. *(BR Western Region Magazine)*

September 1960, the WR Blue Pullman diesel expresses are undergoing their first complete overhauls. The Bristol Pullman which was withdrawn on May 8th, is the first of the three luxury trains to be treated. This express, which runs twice daily on Mondays to Fridays between Bristol and Paddington, has now run over 370,000 miles. (The intermediate service will be extended to Weston-super-Mare from June 15th.) Overhaul of each train will take about six weeks, and will be carried out in Swindon workshops. During this period, a substitute train, consisting of traditional Pullman coaches hauled by a diesel locomotive, will maintain the schedules. On the return to service of the Bristol set, the Birmingham Pullman will be withdrawn, but the South Wales Pullman will not be withdrawn until next year."

This was not the first time that a set had been withdrawn for such maintenance, the Bristol Pullman having been out of service between 26th February and 12th March 1962. On that occasion, though, little advance notice was given, and it has been suggested that this resulted in much chagrin from the regular passengers. The publicity was, therefore, a bold and innovative means of turning a disadvantage into an advantage, and it worked as well! (In 1963, the WR was reported as having no spare bogies for their train sets, but these were on order at the time. There were certainly spares available in 1960, so they must have been used in the interim, possibly in an attempt to overcome riding difficulties.)

In contrast to modern-day behaviour, an incident for which the railway was clearly not responsible warranted a rapid response and minimal disruption to traffic. This was when an unfortunate individual jumped in front of the up Birmingham Pullman at Seer Green. The train continued to Old Oak Common, where the front was quickly washed down, allowing it to continue to Paddington with minimal delay. (An accident also took place on an unreported date, resulting in the death of a platelayer at Uffington, when he was hit by one of the Pullman sets.)

Unlike the LMR, the WR was keen to see maximum utilisation of its trains whenever possible and this sometimes took the form of a special working for VIP clientele. One such was a special from Swansea to Liverpool Aintree for the Grand National on 21st March 1964, but unfortunately exact route details are not known. Doubtless, there were quite a few celebrating on the return journey, for the winner was Team Spirit, ridden by GW Robinson at the attractive odds of 18-1. It has also been suggested that, on 14th April 1963, a charter was arranged on behalf of the Bristol and District Railway Society between Bristol and Plymouth (out via Okehampton, and return via Newton Abbot) but this has not been confirmed. As this was only three days after the date when it is reported that none of the sets was available, its operation should be questioned.

Such success in attracting charter workings was nothing compared with the dilemma that would shortly be facing British Railways and the WR in particular. This was simply what to do with the whole Blue Pullman fleet on completion of the electrification of the LMR route from Euston. This would also spell the end for the Paddington to Birmingham service, the reasons for whose curtailment are discussed in detail shortly. As far as the WR was concerned it would also mean Paddington potentially being in a similar situation to the one they were in in 1960 with just two sets in daily use, although now serving Bristol and Swansea.

As to the question of the future of the two 6-car LMR units, while with hindsight the concentration of all five sets on the WR might seem both simple and obvious, there were definite reasons why such a decision was not

SOUTH WALES PULLMAN

The Blue Pullman service to South Wales commenced in the late summer of 1961, and from the outset there was a daily fill-in of a Paddington to Cardiff return working, the set for which is seen awaiting departure from Cardiff on 5ᵗʰ May 1966.
(A Swain)

Opposite page, top: The curving platforms of Swansea provide the background to this delightful view of the train await-ing departure. It would appear that the destination blind has been altered to suit the newer working, but this cannot be confirmed. The view of the driver in his uniform talking to the lady is delightful, perhaps he was trying to encourage her to travel. A rough estimate of the loading figures for the South Wales service revealed that it was in the order of 130 passengers per train. This appears to be only a 59% loading, but care should be taken using pure statistical information in isolation, as the distance that each passenger travelled, and their class of travel, are not known. Catering on the South Wales services, however, was said to be the most lucrative of all the WR Blue Pullman workings.

Opposite page, bottom: Careful study of the Pullman by what appears to be a steam crew at Swansea High Street on an unrecorded date. Note that the air horns now have a small cover fitted.
(Antony M Ford Collection)

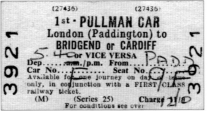
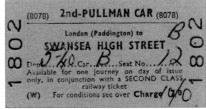

First and second class Pullman supplement tickets for the South Wales route, all of which date from 1966.
(Antony M Ford Collection)

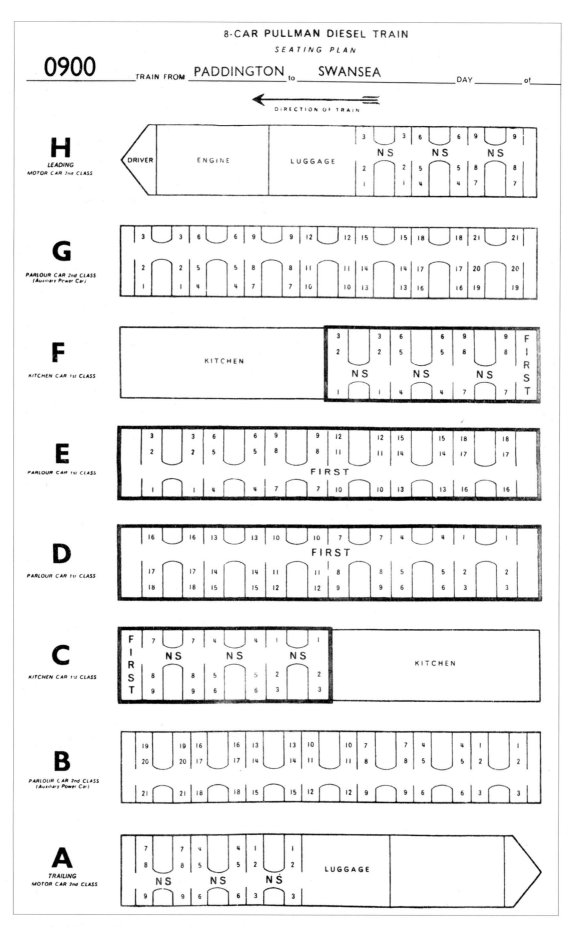

8-CAR PULLMAN DIESEL TRAIN

SEATING PLAN

0900 TRAIN FROM **PADDINGTON** to **SWANSEA** DAY of

DIRECTION OF TRAIN

A rare find by Ian Shawyer was this unused example of the seating plan for the down Swansea service. It would appear that, with minor variations, the same plan could be used for the other WR Pullman services, and it is known that a variation was also used by the LMR. The loadings would be filled out by the conductor, and then handed in at Paddington, for which purpose the office junior was invariably sent to meet the train upon arrival. At a very rough estimate, some 16,000 of these forms must have been completed during the lifetime of the sets on the WR alone, yet this is the only one so far located, and none from the LMR has yet been found.

(Ian Shawyer Collection)

Paddington-bound in Sonning Cutting.   (*Antony M Ford Collection*)

immediately taken, the most important being that to do so could "over-Pullman" a restricted area.

No doubt for this very reason a trial was arranged for 16th October 1965 when one of the Midland sets, consisting of M60090, M60730, M60740, M60741, M60731 and M60091, ran between Leeds and Kings Cross, conveying a party of senior BRB and regional officials. The journey had involved the train running empty from Reddish (Manchester) via Huddersfield, Mirfield, Low Moor and Laisterdyke to Leeds where it was boarded. The run to Kings Cross was scheduled for 2hrs 46min, which included a three-minute stop at Doncaster. An additional three minutes was allowed on the return, with the one stop en-route. Unfortunately, details of the actual timings for the day have not been located.

The reason for this is that the Eastern Region was being pressured to take the two LMR trains, and as late February 1966, this was still the case. In the event, they were despatched to the WR, the reluctance of the ER being due to the riding qualities, although at the same time, Kings Cross was still riding high on the euphoria of their fleet of Deltics, against which everything tended to be viewed with some disdain. It has been suggested by Antony Ford that two further trials involving (it is believed) a 6-car set also took place around this time, one on the North Eastern Region and the other to Harwich. Regrettably, no further information on these runs has been located.

The concern over ride quality was still an important issue at this time, for as mentioned previously, various modifications had been made to the bogies, and after 1962 there are few complaints over the riding to report on, so it is reasonable to assume that despite a settling down of the situation, or an acceptance that the sets were riding as well as they ever would, this was not enough for the ER. The ER main line was perhaps the best maintained in the country, a view supported after 1927, and again in 1967, when as a result of accidents on the SR (Sevenoaks and Hither Green) the ER main line was used to test the riding qualities of the stock involved. In both cases, no fault was found, so suspicion focussed on the SR permanent way. Nevertheless, on this superbly maintained main line, the Blue Pullman sets still misbehaved, so the ER probably used every trick they could to avoid accepting them!

115

BRISTOL PULLMAN

At speed, just west of Wootton Bassett with a Bristol-bound service taking the line via Bath, and shortly to begin the descent to Dauntsey. On the left, the Badminton line can be seen diverging. This was the preferred route for fast Bristol services, including the South Wales Pullman. (PJ Sharpe)

Bristol Temple Meads at 2.55pm, sometime in 1962 (the actual date is not recorded). The 3.15pm service to Paddington has just arrived at the platform, and will call at Bath Spa and Chippenham before its scheduled arrival at Paddington at 5.15pm. (HJ Ashman/Adrian Vaughan Collection)

Passing under clear signals, the down Birmingham service from Paddington approaches High Wycombe on 20th August 1965. To the right, is the branch from Bourne End (closed on 4th May 1970). The Blue Pullman sets were the third type of motive power to operate on the WR that utilised electric transmission, previous ones being the 0-6-0 diesel shunters in the series 15100-7, and the two Gas-Turbine electric engines, 18000 and 18100. *(HK Harman)*

The rear end of an up service at (it is believed) Leamington Spa; the use of the oil tail lamp will be noted. (There does not appear to be any consistency about when these were used, compared with a red filter on the built-in lamp, so perhaps it was simply that one of the latter could not be found.) The destination blind was reversible for up and down workings on the various routes and as a result, the stops always appeared in order. *(PJ Sharpe)*

Before all five came together on the WR, BRB tried one final alternative. In order to tap into a business need, the sets would have to be found work in areas with large conurbations. This ruled out most of the Scottish Region, for example, so the suggested new home was on the Southern Region as a replacement for the locomotive-hauled Bournemouth Belle. It was as if the wheel had turned full circle, as this was similar to the suggestion made by Hugh Barker back in 1954 (see page 1). However, the Southern Region was in some turmoil as work accelerated towards the completion of the Bournemouth electrification scheme, which would result in the abolition of steam from the area, including the existing Bournemouth Belle. (Electrification to Bournemouth was originally scheduled for early 1967, although it was subsequently put back until July 1967.)

Again it was a suggestion destined to come to nothing, as the forceful David McKenna, General Manager at Waterloo, would have nothing to do with a second-hand replacement that was potentially slower than the newer 4REP electric sets that would later be introduced. As the Bournemouth suggestion was only a paper exercise, there is no evidence that any trials took place on the SR. (One set did work from Paddington to Brockenhurst on 25th March 1971, but this was a special.) Waterloo or Paddington to Exeter were other options worth considering in the area, with the latter being perhaps the more likely, but surprisingly, there does not appear to be any reference to this being considered.

It might be worth considering a Blue Pullman running on a similar schedule as existed on the Bournemouth line after July 1967 (Waterloo to Southampton in 70 minutes, and Waterloo to Bournemouth in 100 minutes). The ride endured by passengers for some two decades on the REP and TC stock was lively to say the least, so the thought of a 90mph Pullman on the same line brings positive shudders to mind. "With a Splash" (see page 75) would probably have been replaced by "With a Deluge".

BR was therefore left with little option — the WR it had to be, unless it chose to scrap the units, or sell them

On 17th May 1961, the renowned railway enthusiast and photographer Ivo Peters took a cab-ride from Bath to Paddington. This was the scene as recorded in the cab en-route and with the speedometer reading 90mph. The obligatory pack of cigarettes will be noted.

(Ivo Peters Collection)

on for service elsewhere, and it is not believed that either was seriously considered at this time. Paddington though were nothing short of wary about how best to utilise an asset that had literally been thrust upon them, and as result considerable work was undertaken by the WR Movements Department regarding their future potential. Their remit was economy, from which it was also almost impossible to separate the question of train formation. The paperwork generated behind the scenes at Paddington is accessible at the National Archive, but is superbly described by Paul Metcalfe. (The options are numbered in the following text and the table on page 125 for clarity.)

Opposite page, top: The March 1964 excursion from Swansea to Aintree for the Grand National, seen near the site of the former Collins Green Station.   *(JK Barnett)*

Opposite page, bottom: Saturday 13th March 1965 and the charter of a WR set from Coventry to West Hartlepool for the Rugby Union Championship Final. This was one of two special trains to run between the two locations on that day, the other being steam-hauled by Britannia class 70020 "Mercury". The Pullman unit is seen here at its destination, the furthest north that a Blue Pullman set ever ventured. The crew uniforms are distinctly non-WR! As time passed, the sets also became popular for weekend charter work, and visited locations as diverse as Norwich, Guildford and Carmarthen. The cost for the charter of an 8-car set in 1972 was £1,200, but strangely, it appears that the WR were not always keen to allow the sets to be used for specials. Possibly there were justifiable maintenance reasons for this, as all three trains were in regular use at the time, or it could simply have been politically-inspired inertia by the individual responsible for such charter work, after all, why promote an asset that was, in some respects, a millstone? Another excursion was on 9th March 1968, when a set worked from Bristol to Leeds carrying the Bristol City Football Club players and officials. The prestige train was chartered for the team as they had reached the last 16 of the FA cup. (Bristol City lost the tie 2-0, so the Pullman set was not required again.)   *(IS Carr)*

Paddington on an unreported date and a Pullman devoid of passengers. The fear expressed by the Western Region was that to concentrate all the sets in the one area would risk denuding their first class passengers from other services. But, as explained in the accompanying text, there was really little choice.

"In their report, they list a number of possible arrangements for the 36 cars. It also highlighted the fact that, although there was sufficient motive power and kitchen cars for five trains (options 1 and 2), the possible formations were such that not all of the five sets could run economically at the same time. The best arrangement, they felt, was to produce four trains (options 3, 4 and 5), even though this left two motor and kitchen cars with only limited value as spares. Some of the suggested formations were discounted because of unsuitable class composition or unsuitable seating layout. The best, they decreed, seemed to be an arrangement of four 8-car trains with identical capacities of 108 first class and 114 second class seats, that was six fewer second-class seats than the WR trains had been used to (option 4).

An alternative was to leave the three WR sets as they were, and leave a fourth train of 72 first and 132 second class seats (option 5). Both the alternatives involved a conversion cost of £2,000, and both also involved the use of first class cars as second class, although they were to be separated by the kitchen from those that were to be used for first class.

The report decided (and in this they agreed with decisions made a decade previously) there were three main uses for a Pullman train. The first as an additional service using a completely new path, the second as a replacement of an ordinary train on an existing service or finally, as a stand-by for those Pullmans already in operation. The stand-by option was discounted, and if an additional service was introduced, a Blue Pullman would have to cover its own costs. These costs were quoted as £95,000 a year. They worked out that if the Pullman drew all its traffic from existing services, it would have to carry 190,000 passengers per annum to obtain sufficient in supplements, and food and drink profit, to cover its costs. If 10% of its passengers were new to rail travel, it would have to carry 150,000 persons yearly.

The routes with the highest Pullman potential had been identified as South Wales and Bristol, but the report, carried out before the transfer of the two LMR sets had been undertaken, made it clear that the only hope of employing further Blue Pullmans profitably was to use them to replace existing services instead of additional ones.

But even then, replacing a loco-hauled service would mean the Pullman having to cover an additional cost of between £33,000 and £38,000 a year, depending on whether the existing service had a restaurant car.

To make a profit of £10,000 a year, the Blue Pullman would have to carry some 90,000 passengers from existing services. If 10% of its passengers were new to rail, the figure was reduced to 70,000 a year, but if substituting an existing service for a Pullman made passengers look for other modes of transport, then 110,000 passengers would be needed to make the same profit.

Routes also turned out to be a major headache. Having decided on four train formations, the region decreed that the existing services on the Paddington-Bristol/South Wales routes were already making sufficient money for the region to justify continuing them. They decided that for the remaining train, only three possibilities were really acceptable. Out of these options, the one with the greatest potential for profit was to run a reciprocal service on the Paddington-Bristol route starting from London in the morning. However, they warned that there could be serious problems associated with having such a high proportion of Pullmans on that route. A reciprocal service was also possible for the South Wales service, but once again the risk of going beyond saturation point for the Pullmans was present here too. The third case was the Golden Hind. The plan was to replace the existing train with a Blue Pullman on the South West route. But the existing traffic was, they pointed out, not ideally suited for Pullmans and would probably create a train with a high proportion of second-class accommodation.

Replacement of the Golden Hind was likely, they added, to produce capacity problems on the Mayflower on the same route. But if a Blue Pullman ran profitably on one return run a day on the route it would have been available at marginal cost for a shorter return trip from Paddington in the middle of the day and Paddington to Oxford was suggested. The case for the Golden Hind was somewhat shot down because of the power output of the Pullmans in terms of keeping time, not because of the suggestion they could not get over the banks in Devon. The 8-car set did not have sufficient power to maintain the timings of the Golden Hind at that point and re-diagramming was out of the question, as it would have caused major problems west of Plymouth. Traffic on the Golden Hind was also averaging under 300 passengers a day during the period, and that was insufficient for Pullman operation. The total of first-class passengers on both the Golden Hind and the Mayflower averaged less than 100 in each direction, and on some days it was less than 50. If the Pullman was to be given the Golden Hind then the formation would need to be that which gave it 72 first class and 132 second class seats. The report concluded that the only two feasible uses for the two LMR Pullmans was to provide reciprocal services on the same routes or to replace the Golden Hind. Each of these possibilities required further consideration, however, as at that stage there was not a clear-cut case for any of them."

The matter was formally discussed in BR Headquarters Report Number O77 of May 1965, which undertook, "To examine the problem of determining the best use for the 36 Blue Pullman cars". Like the Paddington options though, the BR report was full on fact and short on solutions, the impression being given that the WR had made a success of its previous Pullman operations and were therefore best placed to succeed again. This may be a little unfair, but by the lack of any mention of it, the various contributors seem to have ignored the fact that the success of the WR was in no small part due to the revenue accrued from the Birmingham service, which was due to

be withdrawn. So now the question can be asked, why was it to be withdrawn?

The answer is that Marylebone and Euston had made what was perhaps a questionable decision to concentrate all London to Birmingham traffic on the newly-electrified former LNWR route from Euston, and at the same time, reduce the former GWR route to secondary status. It should be remembered that this was at a time when alternative or duplicate routes were simply not considered necessary. With hindsight, it would have made sense to retain the Pullman service, and operate it between Birmingham New Street, Coventry and Paddington. Line capacity in the Birmingham area, however, was a problem in addition to the same situation that had occurred when the new trains had been introduced to Bristol in 1960 – a faster service would be available (in this case via the electrified route) with no surcharge to be paid. In the event, the Paddington to Birmingham service subsequently ended on 3rd March 1967.

In reaching its "non-conclusions", BR Report 077 also provides some interesting details relating to expenses at the time. Figures for 1964, the last complete year for which they were available, gives receipts for the trains operating on the WR as £104,000 (South Wales), £134,000 (Bristol) and £157,000 (Birmingham). This was against a total operating cost for all three trains of £95,000, a third of which was maintenance. The result was a gross operating profit of £300,000 - in the order of 76%, an admirable figure, although it does not appear that depreciation had been factored in at this stage.

Report 077 however, only afforded options – not decisions, and the problem of what to do with the trains eventually had to be resolved. To run additional Pullman services on either the Bristol or South Wales route risked saturation, while running the trains on a new route could mean taking away existing revenue, unless it was felt it could generate enough additional "Pullman-type" clientele. One serious consideration (as mentioned by Paul Metcalfe) was to run to Plymouth as a replacement for the Golden Hind, but it was recognised that this would require a greater percentage of second-class accommodation than was then available. A mid-day Paddington to Oxford service was also considered. The report considered that there was no potential for a cross-country service such as Birmingham to South Wales via Gloucester, and if the Blue Pullman was to replace an existing service, there could be problems with limited space for parcels and luggage, so the most likely role for the trains was probably a modern-day Cheltenham Spa Express. (Difficulties with luggage might have ensued if the trains were used for cross-country workings, where experience had shown a greater proportion of luggage was carried.) In a similar vein it might be thought that a premier service to and from Worcester or Hereford might have been considered, but there does not appear to be any record of such thoughts. (Decades later, luggage space seems to have been conveniently ignored by twenty-first century train operators.)

The report also provides useful details about the

One result of the additional sets becoming available was the commencement of the mid-day Oxford service, seen here being ceremoniously flagged away from Paddington on its first day of operation on 5th March 1967. It was hoped that tourism would be the main money spinner for this service, and accordingly, it was targeted at visitors from North America. Air Vice Marshall William Foster MacNeece Foster, the Lord Mayor of Oxford, is seen in charge of proceedings, accompanied by Mr Jack Herfurt, Consul General at the United States Embassy, and Mr David Pattison, BR(WR) London Division Manager. Other guests on the first run included the London Manager of the American Express organisation and representatives of nine travel agencies. On arrival at Oxford, the party's tour of several colleges was followed by a civic reception at the Town Hall.

(British Railways)

Below: The down Oxford Pullman speeding through Radley, formerly the junction for the short branch to Abingdon. Close inspection of the photograph shows that the crew are attired in conventional uniforms.

(RHG Simpson)

Following the transfer of the LMR sets to the Western Region, some crew training was necessary, often between Paddington and Westbury. This was not a route used regularly by the trains, but route knowledge was required for Old Oak Common and Bristol Pullman link crews as a potential diversion. Here, a 6-car set, complete with full yellow warning panel on the front, passes westbound through Newbury on a wet November day in 1966. At this stage, the Midland Pullman title still remains on the vehicle sides. *(EC Paine Ltd)*

timescale for major overhauls and repairs, which involved a complete train being out of service for some seven weeks every time general repairs were required (between 36 and 48 months in service). The same report spoke of a main engine overhaul taking place every 9 to 12 months, which would seem to be a good case for having at least one spare engine available. Repairs to the auxiliary diesel engine were scheduled for every 18 months.

The advantage of running just four sets was that with two spare motor coaches (albeit first class) a train could be released from repair earlier, while if only three sets were in regular operation, the stand-by train could possibly be used at weekends, although the traffic potential was small. Whatever variation on a theme was chosen, it would still mean that part of an asset would be underutilised, which itself echoed the position of the LMR in trying to find special traffic for the Midland Pullman.

For the first time, the report dealt with depreciation, and this gives some idea about the initial capital cost involved. The cost of the units in 1960 was put at £1,662,000, and spares at £336,092 (presumably not cor-

rected for inflation to 1965). This related to the 36 vehicles, but presumably not the cost of new workshop facilities, shore supplies, and so on. Depreciation was quoted as £31,000 per annum. (In 1960 it was said to be £11,250, and the larger figure is taken from the WR report on 1964 train receipts, so it is not clear whether the increased depreciation figure was simply an adjustment for inflation, or a means of deliberately reducing the time taken to write off their capital cost.) Assuming each set to be roughly the same value (and not taking into account the variations in depreciation of a 6- or 8-car train), it can be said that the expected minimum "book" life of the trains was just under 13 years, this being the time needed to write off their original cost. This timescale should not be regarded as the length of their useful lives, but ironically, they would just about achieve this 13-year lifespan. BR also identified that the sets had a relatively small scrap value, and only a few minor components were capable of being re-used in other trains, so the WR really was in a corner, with no option but to retain the trains in some form or another for the foreseeable future.

An official view of power car M60090 at Swindon with the front painted "for visual effect". The date is recorded as 4th July 1966.
(British Railways)

By comparison, ordinary train stock in a pool of similar vehicles depreciated at £20,000 annually. The operating cost of a Blue Pullman was understandably higher, and included the cost of travelling technicians, so a suggestion was made that these men be replaced by "Platform Inspectors" although it is not confirmed whether this actually took place.

Something in favour of the Blue Pullmans was that their fuel and lubricant costs were lower than a comparative train, although this might have been because the cost comparisons were based on 255 days use per year for the Pullman, compared with 307 for an ordinary train.

Within the reports, the following set permutations were referred to (it will be noted that the only common vehicle between the WR and LMR sets was the Parlour First). References to bogie types are described in Appendix A.

Table 1A: Original formations					
Type	**Seats**	**Bogies**	**WR**	**LMR**	**Running numbers**
1 – Motor 2nd	18	A – B	6		60094–60099
2 – Parlour 2nd	42	C – D	6		60644–60649
3 – Kitchen 1st	18	Trailer – Trailer	6		60734–60739
4 – Parlour 1st	36	Trailer – Trailer	6	4	60740–60749
5 – Kitchen 1st	18	C – Trailer		4	60730–60733
6 – Motor 1st	12	A – B		4	60090–60093

Table 1B: Original allocations					
Train	**Car Types**	**Seating 1st**	**Seating 2nd**	**Total**	**Original Allocation**
A	1-2-3-4-4-3-2-1	108	120	228	WR
B	1-2-3-4-4-3-2-1	108	120	228	WR
C	1-2-3-4-4-3-2-1	108	120	228	WR
D	6-5-4-4-5-6	132	-	132	LMR
E	6-5-4-4-5-6	132	-	132	LMR

Train	Car Types	Seating 1st	Seating 2nd	Total
Table 2: Options and permutations				
Option 1				
A	1-2-3-4-4-5-6*	108	72	180
B	1-2-3-4-4-5-6*	108	72	180
C	1-2-3-4-4-5-6*	108	72	180
D	1-2-3-4-4-5-6*	108	72	180
E	1-2-3-4-4-3-2-1	108	120	228
Option 2				
A	1-2-3-4-4-3-2-6*	108	114	222
B	1-2-3-4-4-5-2-6*	108	114	22
C	1-2-3-4-4-5-1	108	78	186
D	1-2-3-4-4-5-1	108	78	186
E	6-5-4-4-5-6	132	-	132
Option 3				
A	1-2-3-4-4-3-2-6*	108	114	222
B	1-2-3-4-4-3-2-6*	108	114	222
C	1-2-3-4-4-4-5-1	144	78	222
D	1-2-3-4-4-4-5-1	144	78	222
Option 4				
A	1-2-3-4-4-3-2-6*	108	114	222
B	1-2-3-4-4-3-2-6*	108	114	222
C	1-2-3-4-4-5-4*-1	108	114	222
D	1-2-3-4-4-5-4*-1	108	114	222
Option 5				
A	1-2-3-4-4-3-2-1	108	120	228
B	1-2-3-4-4-3-2-1	108	120	228
C	1-2-3-4-4-3-2-1	108	120	228
D	6*4*5*-4-4-5*-4*-6*	72	132	204
* Indicates the first class cars that would have been downgraded to second class.				

For the final three options, four spare vehicles would result, two of type 6 and two of type 5.

While all of these were innovative suggestions, there were also drawbacks. Option 1 would have meant that unless an original 228-seat set were used on the Bristol or South Wales services, the reduction in second class seating capacity could have led to insufficient accommodation for 230-240 days a year on the up services, and 130 days a year for the return down journeys. With a loss of revenue put at £20,000 per annum, this plan was abandoned.

One note of optimism was that if just four sets were operating (in whatever combination) the two spare motor coaches, albeit first class, would allow a train to be released from repair earlier, and if only three sets were in regular operation, the stand-by train could possibly be used at weekends, although the likely traffic potential was small. Whichever variation on this theme was chosen, it would still mean part of an asset being under-used, and this exactly echoed the position that the LMR had faced years earlier, with little traffic ever being found for the Midland Pullman in the form of special workings.

All the remaining options suffered similar disadvantages in lacking sufficient accommodation. Option 4 would have required some relatively major expenditure, either in running additional power cables or making bogie changes involving traction motors. Additionally, there would be a need for alterations to the springing of the bogies. The alternative, had this option been chosen, would have been to have power bogies on vehicles that were not adjacent to each other.

The final analysis also gave details of the profits

PULLMAN LIVERY

Opposite page, top: Platform 4 at Paddington on 13th March 1968, with the down South Wales Pullman about to depart. Blue and grey colours dominate the scene.

(G Cooper)

Opposite page, bottom: Busy times at Paddington in the late afternoon. No date is given but it is circa 1967; the platform boards are typical for the period, and guide the passenger towards the South Wales Pullman (left) and Bristol Pullman (right).

(CT Gifford)

Right: In the opinion of many, the necessary addition of jumper cables to the front ends was one of the worst aesthetic decisions to affect the former six-car sets. The result is seen at Old Oak Common on 14th February 1967, with the cut-away between the buffers (necessary for permanent access to the coupling) also visible. Note that the sets were only joined by a conventional screw coupling.

(A Swain)

Below: A rare glimpse inside the Pullman shed at Old Oak Common on 3rd October 1967, with the power car of a WR set, W60098, displaying the new livery of the time. This black and white image does not fully do justice to the intrusion of the yellow end. As is well known, the smart appearance of the new paint lasted little more than a few days.

(R Bird)

127

made from the supplementary fare and on-train catering for each service:

Service	Average supplement	Food and drink profit per passenger
Bristol Pullman	7s 4d	1s 11d
Birmingham Pullman	7s 4d	2s 8d
South Wales Pullman	7s 4d	3s 9d

The higher profit margin on the South Wales service reflected the greater distance travelled, although, in truth, it was not greatly different from the distance travelled by the Bristol Pullman.

After all this debate, the eventual decision was to concentrate all five sets on the WR, and make what was publicly described as an "expansion" of the Pullman operation, which took the form of running a 12-car Pullman service from Bristol to Paddington in the morning and a similar 12-car return run in the evening. This would involve operating the former LMR 6-car sets in multiple, and accordingly, they were modified (it is believed at Swindon) with jumper cables at the ends, the bodywork between the buffers cut away to facilitate the permanent fitting of a screw coupling and the air horns relocated beneath the left-hand buffer. As will be seen from the accompanying photographs, these changes did nothing to enhance the trains' previous neat appearance. In August and November 1966, respectively, the two sets were transferred from Swindon (where they had been in store since their arrival from the LMR) to Old Oak Common for crew-training purposes. Clearly, the WR appeared to be in no great hurry to effect the transfer, and indeed, they remained on the books of the LMR until March 1967.

On arrival at Paddington from Bristol in the morning, the two 6-car sets would divide with one making a mid-day return run to Oxford, covering the 63.5 miles via Didcot in one hour, start to stop, while the other would do a mid-day turn to Bristol, and on the 1.15pm return jour-

Trailer Parlour First, No W60747, in revised livery on 31ˢᵗ October 1967. Of note is the continuation of the colour scheme around the vehicle ends, as well as the vertical centre line at the windows.   *(Antony M Ford Collection)*

In service in the new livery at Bristol Temple Meads. The lunchtime 1.15pm departure for Paddington is seen leaving on 19th July 1968. Not possible to illustrate with still photographs is the use of one of the Pullman sets for a series of adverts for ladies lingerie around this time.
(G Roy Hounsell)

ney would call at Swindon, giving the Wiltshire town its first regular Pullman service. (Shades of the pre-war Cheltenham Spa working perhaps, and in this respect almost the only suggestion from the 1965 report that was actually converted into practice.)

This still left the original three WR 8-car sets, and it was decided to use one as an additional working on the South Wales service, so that there would be morning and evening trains each way on the route. The third 8-car set would be held in reserve, presumably at Old Oak Common. Later still, a mid-day Paddington to Cardiff and return working was introduced using an 8-car formation, but it is not clear whether this used the spare set, or the one that had worked up from Swansea in the morning. Shortly afterwards, a reverse direction working was introduced to Bristol using an 8-car set down in the morning and up in the evening. This meant that all five sets could be in use daily, but there was then no spare capacity at all, as at the same time, the WR ridded itself of the loco-hauled "Wells Fargo" sets, most of which were then scrapped. Details of any substitutions are not known, but they were obviously covered by standard loco-hauled stock.

Before any of these changes could take place, there

was a need for additional crews, so training on the former Midland Pullmans began between Paddington and West-bury in late 1966. It has been suggested that around this time, a trial took place between Bristol and Plymouth, possibly as a prelude to a regular Plymouth working discussed in the earlier proposals, and no doubt intended to assess the performance of the sets on the steep South Devon banks. However, this trial cannot be confirmed.

The suitability of the units to maintain schedules on the Plymouth services might excuse a slight digression at this stage. On the WR the weight of a full 8-car diesel Pullman set, with a power output of 2,000hp, was in the order of 358 tons, which was also the maximum trailing weight allowed for the WR 2,000hp diesel-hydraulic loco-motives of the D6xx and D8xx classes over the steepest part of the banks (although here, the weight of the loco-motive was not included). The same limit also applied to King class steam engines over the same stretch. The weight quoted for the Pullman was empty, but even if a complement of passengers was added, the weight would only come up to perhaps 380 tons or more - still less than a locomotive plus its rake of coaches. The caution displayed by Paddington, therefore, in stating they did not consider the units suitable for use over this stretch on the

An up service from either Bristol or South Wales, on the through line at Reading in 1968. To the left is an SR electric unit on the service to Redhill. By this time, female staff (referred to as "attendants") were working alongside the men, although it is known that on the up trains the crews would apparently disappear at Reading, and service to passengers was almost non-existent thenceforth to Paddington. (David Wittamore/Kidderminster Railway Museum)

Opposite page top: The 12-car service operating on the Bristol route, seen here west of Chippenham. Of necessity, some of the original first-class seating had been downgraded to second, each unit now carrying a maximum 72 first- and 60 second-class passengers. Towards the end, some swapping of power cars occurred. Evidence suggests that, although there was no reason why it should not have been the other way round, it was the LMR cars that were substituted onto the former WR sets, perhaps causing havoc with seating. With four power cars in the 12-car formation, the likelihood of total engine failure was remote (as it had been with having two power cars in the original formation); this would later be an advantage with the HST sets. (David Wittamore/Kidderminster Railway Museum)

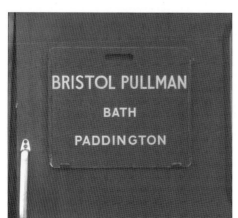

Opposite page, bottom: For a while, the ex-Midland Pullman sets were used for crew training on the Berks and Hants line, and on race days, they were sometimes used for members as a first class only train. One such working is seen at Newbury Racecourse on 24th April 1974. (DE Canning)

Left: During the final years, a slight modification was made to the body sides of the former LMR six-car sets to allow the inclusion of the then-standard metal descriptive panel. It also saved the expense of adding the familiar indicator blinds to the Guard's compartments.

An unusual special working sponsored by Ian Allan Travel. The location is Basingstoke, and the working is an evening special from London (Paddington) to Brockenhurst, where a coach transfer took place to Beaulieu Abbey for a medieval banquet, marketed as "Dinner with a Difference". This is thought to have been a one-off, occurring late in the life of the sets on 25th March 1971. The sound of the Blue Pullman trains (engine noise, followed by quiet, and then engine noise again) would not be heard again at Basingstoke for almost 20 years when HSTs became familiar on the cross-country workings. The dirty roof of the unit, which was typical of the later livery, is unfortunately rather obvious.

basis of scheduling alone, is perhaps a little difficult to understand. A 6-car diesel Pullman set would also have had an even better power to weight ratio, of course.

A 6-car set did work to Plymouth on 24th December 1970, but as a special in connection with the opening of a new hotel in the City. It returned empty, but with the addition of a pilot over the South Devon banks in the form of a Western class diesel-hydraulic. A few days later, the return special ran from London to Plymouth and return on 28th December. This was also formed of a 6-car set, and was again piloted over the same section. There was some credence then, to the assertion by BR engineers that the units were "technically unsuitable" to deal with the South Devon banks. (The photograph by David Canning reproduced on the opposite page appeared in the *Classic Diesels & Electrics* article referred to in Chapter 5.)

Apart from the mechanical modifications to the

ends of the former LMR trains, aesthetically too the units were changing. The Pullman logo was now considered outmoded, and the decision was taken to radically alter the external paintwork, basically to the reverse of what it had been previously. Jack Howe was not in favour of this revised colour scheme, and he tried to have the same Nanking Blue livery applied to the Mark 2 Pullman stock, unsuccessfully as it turned out. Additionally, yellow ends were provided; some of these changes are easily identified in the accompanying illustrations.

At first, there were considerable variations to the yellow applied to the ends of the power cars, not all details of which are known. One of the former LMR power cars is known to have had the driver's doors painted yellow, with the colour extending to the bottom of the cab. It has been suggested that the painting was probably carried out while the set was in store, and that it was in this form when transferred to the WR. It is believed that both LMR

On 28th December 1970, a special working visited Plymouth from London, and is captured here on its return, the photographer having travelled down especially to capture the rare event on film.

One of the Berks and Hants crew-training trips is seen here, photographed on 25th June 1974 at the site of the Aldermaston troughs at Sun Hill.

(Both: DE Canning)

sets ended their days on the Midland painted externally in exactly the same way as when they began in 1960. Additionally, as befitted their new role, the former LMR sets had the word "Midland" obliterated from their sides, although they still retained their coach numbers prefixed by the letter "M". Interestingly, it was suggested that MKFL (Motor Kitchen First with Lavatory) 60730 from the original Midland Pullman Set 1, had acquired the prefix "NE", but this has not been confirmed.

Full repainting of the first set was dealt with at Swindon, and involved an 8-car train that was undergoing overhaul at the time. The new livery was basically a reversal of the original colours, having white bodies with a band of blue the depth of the windows. Unfortunately, the white weathered very quickly, and a dismal grey re-sulted. Internally, the cars also received a face-lift, with seat covers and carpets renewed, and the interior décor of the first-class accommodation coming into line with the contemporary Mark 2 Pullman fleet. In this form, the re-launched train was seen first on the South Wales service. All the other sets were similarly dealt with when they were at Swindon for overhaul. At the same time all the power cars, except W60095 and W60099, were fitted with dual WR and BR AWS, the exceptions being fitted with the original WR contact system only.

An article by Adrian Curtis in the July 2002 issue of *Traction* magazine, confirms details of the formal allocations in January 1967, with both former LMR 6-car sets being based at Bristol Bath Road. W60094, W60095, W60644, W60645, W60734, W60735, W60745 and

| BRITISH RAILWAYS | CAR/ LOCO No. *60'36* | HOME DEPOT | BR, 33063 | C/W |
| | DEPOT WHERE LEFT | | **Y 62456** | |

DATE *26th Nov 71* TIME

REPORTED BY *R R Maclye*   DEPOT *CMREX*

DEFECTS. Leave a clear line between items	ACTION TAKEN BY M'TCE STAFF	CHECK or DEPOT No.	S.M.'s or H. & M.
PANTRY FLOOR DRAIN CAP MISSING DANGEROUS TO FEMALE STAFF WITH HIGH HEELS	New cover 3036 fitted		
STAFF COMPARTMENT CONDUCTOR'S TABLE MUST BE REFITTED.			

SIGNATURE of SUPERVISOR .... DATE .... TIME .... DEPOT ....

An example from a driver's fault book, rescued from a condemned unit at Old Oak Common. Defects would include both mechanical and vehicle items, with several within the record appearing to be due simply to age of the units. Not all could be repaired locally, and initially, it appears that both Derby and Swindon shared the maintenance, as well as the necessary modifications of the WR sets. Certainly, this applied in 1961, when a set destined for the WR at Swindon was routed south from Birmingham via Stourbridge Junction and Cheltenham on 25th November. By 1971, certain defects were apparently left unattended, although those relating to driver comfort (the cab heater and draughts, for example) were often reported several times, as a matter of personal priority. (Neil Ruffles)

W60746 were at Newport (Ebbw Junction) and the remaining two WR sets were at Old Oak Common. The Newport allocation is somewhat strange, but might have been on paper only, as it is believed that the Welsh set was still actually stabled at Swansea.

In this form, the five sets entered the final period of their working lives, and possibly the most noteworthy item affecting any of the trains was in the summer of 1968, when Mr Peter Hughes of Buntingford hired an 8-car WR Pullman set to convey guests from Paddington to Weston-super-Mare for his son's wedding, his intention being to avoid the guests being penalised by the recently introduced breathalyser test for motorists. For the occasion, the entrance to Platform 6 at Paddington was especially decorated, and a red carpet was unrolled beside the train; four cooks and 14 stewards attended to the 200 guests. Also on the WR, one set was photographed at Newbury racecourse at around this time, presumably on a special working. On other occasions, a number of special workings took place, which involved the trains venturing far off the WR, including the Southern Region and onto previously uncovered LMR metals. Possibly, the most unusual was a trip from Surbiton to Newcastle Emlyn, which took place on 25th April 1970.

Ironically, details of workings over the final years have been more difficult to locate, and it has been sug-

gested by Adrian Curtis that, at times, the WR reverted to 8-car operation for much of the time, with an interchange of certain vehicles between the former LMR and WR sets. If this is correct, it could lead to a considerable list of tabulated information! Some doubt originates from a BR memo of 6th December 1968, when the Paddington General Manager, J Bonham-Carter, suggested the formation of a 7-car set that would have been achieved by inserting an additional Parlour First into each of the existing 6-car trains, which would then take turns to have heavy repairs at six-monthly intervals from May 1969.

The suggestion of a 7-car train was circulated to the Catering Department who, while recognising the difficulties, were far from convinced that this was the best option. Instead, they suggested adjusting the workings so that an 8-car train was used.

An interesting fact to come from British Transport Hotels Ltd within the same correspondence concerns the profit made from catering on the diesel Pullmans. This had clearly dropped, compared with previous years, as the comment was made that, "from a pure catering viewpoint they lose money, and only the addition of 50% of the supplementary fare makes them viable". From the same report, it appears that industrial unrest was still a consideration: "We do have trouble working the Western Region Pullmans; staff are not keen to accept positions on them

Flexible to the end. A former LMR power car on what appears to be a WR 8-car train is recorded near Kensal Green.
(Peter Dobson)

and consequently, they are run with men below the standard we would choose to employ on what should be our best services. 68 staff are required to work the South Wales runs and 28 for the Bristol workings, and there would be some redundancy in the event of the withdrawal of the Pullmans."

It is believed that the eventual outcome was to maintain the *status-quo*, and an 8-car set (with a resulting loss of accommodation) was used on the morning up and evening down Bristol turns when required. This type of set, of course, was what had been originally been used on the Bristol turns. How this affected intended patronage (and similarly, how the running of the 12-car formation had affected patronage, if at all) is not reported. Regardless, there were no doubt some Bristol punters who appreciated being able to pay second-class Pullman prices, yet travel in what had been first-class accommodation.

However, such advantage could not last forever, and behind the scenes, the WR had started a discussion with BRB over the long-term future of the sets, and this was not assisted by the changes in the timetable from May 1969. These changes saw the curtailment of the Oxford service, as well as the other midday fill-in workings to Bristol and Cardiff and the morning Paddington to Bristol and evening Bristol to Paddington workings. No doubt these withdrawals were based on pure economics, although it is known for certain that the Oxford service had been the least well patronised of the three.

All that was left was a morning up Pullman from Bristol, and the corresponding down working in the evening. A similar situation existed with the South Wales service, although here the up and down workings both operated in the morning and the evening. A total of just three sets was therefore required for these services.

The diesel Pullman sets were now unquestionably living on borrowed time. Technological progress and engineering development meant that a number of their previously innovative features were now somewhat dated, while in addition, the cost of maintaining a fleet of just five individual train-sets was, doubtless, a major consideration, even if no figures have been located. Only three sets were now required, and they were mainly operating a single return run each.

One of the principal difficulties was the promise of air-conditioned Mark 2 locomotive-hauled coaching stock just around the corner (the Mark 2E and Mark 2F vehicles), while slightly further ahead, the APT and HST sets were in the offing. All these were intended to afford far faster and more comfortable travel to the masses, and it was unlikely that the business clientele (which was the main market for the Pullman) would continue to support a service that was both more expensive and also potentially slower – as well as rougher to ride in! Again, therefore, the same situation occurred as when the sets were introduced on the WR in 1960, with comparisons being made with the Bristolian.

135

The two former LMR sets joined together, at the western end of Box Tunnel, with the train heading for Bath and Bristol.
(David Wittamore/Kidderminster Railway Museum)

Inevitably, a formal announcement of the pending withdrawal of the trains the following year was made on 20th November 1972. There was also a run-down on maintenance (which had probably been going on for some time anyway) so that when the final date eventually came, not all the sets were still serviceable. Full details of the actual situation are given in the next chapter.

Regular services ended on Friday 4th May 1973, but there was a remarkable special on the next day. This was to be the final run, and was marketed by BR as an "Enthusiasts' Safari". Paddington were clearly aware of the potential for revenue from the enthusiast at this time, and this Blue Pullman special was just one of a number of officially organised enthusiast specials. (Coincidentally another official special at around the same time had constituted the last trains on the Lambourn branch, and these were also hugely successful.)

The "Safari" was advertised for a price of £10 to include all meals, and it was apparently well-filled with enthusiasts. Departure from Paddington Platform 1 was at 8.53am, and the train ran via High Wycombe to Banbury and Leamington Spa. Thence it ran via the former LNWR single-line route to Kenilworth and Coventry, and on to Birmingham New Street. After this, it travelled via

Cheltenham Spa, Bristol Temple Meads, Severn Tunnel Junction to its eventual destination at Swansea (2.19pm arrival, 5.10pm departure). The return was via Cardiff (with a 3-minute stop for a crew change), Newport, Bristol Parkway, Didcot and Slough to Paddington. The itinerary was such that it encompassed elements of all the former WR routes that were operated by the trains when in general service.

The final leg from Swansea saw the train arrive six minutes late at Newport, but some fast running resulted in an arrival at Paddington at 8.02pm, 18 minutes earlier than the scheduled 8.20pm. The train ran at an average speed of 81mph from Newport, and no less than 88mph between Swindon and Reading! Whether or not this had been intended by BR was a moot point, but it was an excellent bit of marketing for the period. After arrival at Paddington, the passengers de-trained and the set left (it is believed) for Old Oak Common. This was the final time a diesel Pullman would ever be seen at Paddington.

Train Times and Reporting Numbers
Due to changes in the WR services from 1960 to 1967, the various departure times and reporting numbers are best summarised in tabular form:

Up Trains				
Service	**Dates**	**Departure Time**	**Reporting Number**	**Notes**
ex-Bristol	12-9-1960 to 10-9-1961	7.45am	1A00	
ex-Bristol	12-9-1960 to 10-9-1961	12.30pm	1A50	
ex-Wolverhampton Low Level	12-9-1960 to 10-9-1961	7.00am	1A01	
ex-Birmingham Snow Hill	12-9-1960 to 10-9-1961	2.30pm	1A78	
ex-South Wales	11-9-1961 to 8-9-1963	6.40am	1A06	
ex-Bristol	9-9-1963 to 14-6-1964	8.15am	1A14	
ex-Bristol	9-9-1963 to 14-6-1964	3.15pm	1A83	
ex-South Wales	9-9-1963 to 14-6-1964	6.50am	1A11	
ex-Wolverhampton Low Level	9-9-1963 to 14-6-1964	1.00pm	1A55	
ex-Weston-super-Mare	15-6-1964 to 13-6-1965	2.50pm	1A66	
ex-Wolverhampton Low Level	15-6-1964 to 5-3-1967	7.00am	1V02	Ceased to run after this date
ex-Wolverhampton Low Level	15-6-1964 to 5-3-1967	1.00pm	1V16	Ceased to run after this date
ex-Bristol	14-6-1965 to 5-3-1967	8.15am	1A10	
ex-Bristol	14-6-1965 to 5-3-1967	1.15pm	1A50	
ex-South Wales	14-6-1965 to 5-3-1967	6.55am	1A11	
ex-South Wales	14-6-1965 to 5-3-1967	2.30pm	1A64	

Down Trains				
Service	**Dates**	**Departure Time**	**Reporting Number**	**Notes**
to Bristol	12-9-1960 to 10-9-1961	10.05am	1B07	
to Bristol	12-9-1960 to 10-9-1961	4.55pm	1B17	
to Birmingham Snow Hill	12-9-1960 to 10-9-1961	12.10pm	1H13	
to Wolverhampton Low Level	12-9-1960 to 10-9-1961	4.50pm	1H30	
to Bristol	11-6-1961(?) to 14-6-1964	12.45pm	1B13	1B15 from 18-6-1962
to Bristol	11-6-1961(?) to 5-3-1967	5.45pm	1B25	
to South Wales	11-9-1961 to 8-9-1963	4.45pm	1F60	
to South Wales	9-9-1963 to 14-6-1964	4.40pm	1F60	
to Birmingham Snow Hill	9-9-1963 to 14-6-1964	10.10am	1H09	
to Wolverhampton Low Level	9-9-1963 to 14-6-1964	4.50pm	1H30	
to Weston-super-Mare	15-6-1964 to 13-6-1965	11.45am	1B13	
to South Wales	15-6-1964 to 5-3-1967	11.00am	1T32	
to South Wales	15-6-1964 to 13-6-1965	5.40pm	1F60	
to Birmingham Snow Hill	15-6-1964 to 5-3-1967	10.10am	1M11	Ceased to run after this date
to Wolverhampton Low Level	15-6-1964 to 5-3-1967	4.50pm	1M21	Ceased to run after this date
to Bristol	14-6-1965 to 5-3-1967	10.45am	1B10	
to Cardiff General	14-6-1965 to 5-3-1967	11.00am	1F60	

Chapter 7

THE INEVITABILITY OF PROGRESS

Before drawing conclusions solely on the evidence presented in the preceding chapters, it is necessary to return briefly to February 1969, at which time it should be remembered, the Blue Pullman trains (or should they have been called Grey Pullmans at this stage?) had been in service less than nine years, and still had a further five years of running ahead.

On 24th February, the first step in the eventual withdrawal of the units took place in the form of a memorandum from the WR General Manager, J Bonham-Carter at Paddington to the BRB. It was specifically addressed to the Chief Operating Manager, Chief Passenger Manager, Chief Engineer and Rolling Stock Manager, and copies were circulated to other senior interested parties including the General Manager of British Transport Hotels.

The memorandum ("report" would perhaps be a better word as it ran to four closely-typed sides) first described the history of the sets, and then the set the scene for what was to come:

"To assess the value of the Pullman in relation to ordinary services, market research has been carried out. This has shown, clearly, that the Pullman service has no special influence on the majority of our customers' mode of travel; they would travel by train in any event. In fact, there is evidence to suggest that some, who had travelled Second Class Pullman, would have travelled First Class in a traditional service running at Pullman time. (The report added that, "Copies of the Market Survey are available at BRB Headquarters") It is also particularly relevant that there is now little difference in the general standard of comfort between Pullman and the latest type of conventional coaching stock, apart from the facility of meals being served at all seats and air-conditioning being provided in the Pullman. *(Given that the ride of the Blue Pullmans remained the same, this hardly says a lot for the Mark 2 stock of the period!)* If the Pullman services were withdrawn, catering arrangements on the replacement services would require examination to ensure adequate facilities were available, depending upon the time of day. In other words, it might be sensible to have a "reserved seat in the restaurant car" situation on particular trains, and a "fluid service" on others. Equivalent schedules on the same timings as those for the present Pullman services could be covered by the rearrangement of engine and coach workings with the addition of one Type 4 locomotive and nine Mark 2 coaches. In view of all the foregoing considerations, the financial case for withdrawing the Pullman units and replacing them by conventional stock of the newest type has been examined...the most advantageous course financially to be the complete withdrawal of the Pullmans

in May 1970."

The report continued with an assessment of the likely financial impact on revenue, and concluded that the overall loss in revenue annually was likely to be in the order of only £3,190. There was no mention, at this time, of savings on maintenance having been considered. But even if the financial case was strong, Paddington did display an amount of regret over their conclusions:

"The (WR) Board have reached this conclusion with considerable regret because of the "modern image" of the units and the fact that they have been in service for only nine years. The Board also appreciate that, if the proposal to withdraw is adopted, there will be a great deal of criticism of one sort and another, and the matter would, therefore, have to be handled very specially, with extreme care from a Public Relations point of view. Criticism will undoubtedly come from regular passengers who like the Pullman, although they would continue to travel by rail if the units were withdrawn, and no doubt there would be some criticism of the Board for scrapping relatively new equipment."

The report concluded with the view that it was unlikely that another region would be prepared to take over the trains, and in this Paddington were, no doubt, correct. As mentioned elsewhere, this had been found to be impractical in 1966, and it would surely be impossible in 1969. It was now up to the British Railways Board to have the final say, their decision having some degree of urgency, due to the necessary forward planning for the 1970/1 timetable.

Less than two weeks later, on 7th March 1969, the BRB met to consider the WR's request. Six members of the board were present; the meeting was chaired by Mr WO Reynolds, and was attended by Messrs DM Howes, G Crabtree, TCB Miller, GT Smithyman and PB Johnson. Also present, representing the WR, were Messrs TR Barron, S Ridgway, and J Palette.

The case for withdrawal was first outlined by Mr Barron, who also outlined the capital cost of the trains, presumably including their associated spares and shore/servicing facilities as the cost was put at £2.6 million. Allowing for depreciation to date, it was estimated that the amount to be written off was in the order of £1 million. No decision was made at this time, the only comment being that the Chairman would discuss the matter with other BRB officers, while recognising the need for an early decision.

At this stage, though, matters become somewhat convoluted, and it is interesting to try and unravel what might have been going on behind the scenes. There is no other correspondence from the WR or BRB over the

Opposite page: Royal Oak, and the obvious transition from steam. A Paddington-bound WR Pullman unit is seen passing a 49xx/59xx series Hall class locomotive engaged in shunting. Alongside, a Metropolitan line underground train begins its descent ready to dive under the main running lines on its journey to Hammersmith. *(WHR Godwin)*

Without doubt, the loss of the Birmingham service robbed the WR of its most lucrative Pullman operation, and despite every effort by Paddington, the various alternatives did little to fully compensate. In the days then when Snow Hill saw the prestige service, an 8-car set is captured at the station sometime in 1961. (*Michael Mensing*)

planned withdrawal at this time, and as is well known, the trains continued in service for another four years through to 1973. One possibility is that the proposed introduction of Mark 2 stock on the WR was delayed, but this is not known for certain.

Matters were moving in a totally unexpected direction elsewhere, prompted by the desire to see if alternative uses might be found for the sets. The answer was not to be found on BR, and so began (apparently on 18th August 1970) a series of correspondence from BR Engineering Ltd (BREL) in which there is a discussion about the possible sale of all five sets to Yugoslavia; whether the initial approach was made by that country or by BR, is not recorded. Similarly, there is a suggestion that, at some stage, Greece was seen as a possible future home, although no further information has been located on this.

As would be expected, any possible sale would hinge on cost, BREL basing their sale figures loosely on the anticipated production cost of the future HST train sets, together with the write-off value of the Blue Pullmans. This latter amount was quoted by BREL to be still just over £1 million at the end of 1970, clearly showing how inflation had now started to play a part in costings compared with 1969. (More than 18 months had passed since the WR had quoted a write-off figure of the same amount, and without inflation, the write-off figure would be expected to decrease.)

In addition to the £1 million that it was hoped to recoup from a potential purchaser, a further £200,000 was added to cover the necessary modifications, refurbishment and repainting, while the additional of a 25% profit margin resulted in a total sale price of "approximately £1.5 million". (By comparison, the 1973 scrap value of all the trains was put at just £48,000.)

Internal discussions in BR appear to have dragged on, but it was noted that in October 1970, negotiations with a purchaser were about to commence, and it was hoped that these would lead to the WR releasing the stock for the necessary "overhaul and modification" in the spring of 1971 (this was the first time the word "overhaul" had been used). More importantly, perhaps, the correspondence also noted that a figure as low as £1 million in total might be accepted, but this was also said to be the absolute minimum. There was also a hope that this sale would lead to further sales of new stock in later years, but this is not expanded upon.

Regrettably, this was the end of any discussion on the matter, and for whatever reason, no deal was ever struck. However, it could be that the very fact that there was a sale in the offing actually resulted in the trains remaining in service longer than had been intended, as vandalism and decline were more likely to take place if they

A former LMR 6-car set is seen broadside from the Keynsham by-pass on 5th April 1970. This was reported to be the down morning service to Bristol, which was formed of half of the 12-car set that had been used for the earlier up Bristol working (the other 6-car set did the midday fill-in to Oxford). Notice that only the single word "PULLMAN" now appears on the side of the power car. (J Fowler)

were stored awaiting a decision. It will be necessary to return to the topic of storage later.

There is now an unfortunate gap in the surviving paper records until 5th November 1971, during which time it is reasonable to assume that the weight of evidence was sufficient to withdraw them. But without any evidence, the reason for the continuing survival of the Blue Pullman sets must be questioned, and indeed on 5th November, a note from H Jones, the BRB Executive Director for Finance referred to an earlier note of 2nd November (which has not been found) that implied that there had been another proposal for the withdrawal of the trains by the WR.

Matters regarding any final decision appear to have stalled again, although clearly the impasse could not last indefinitely, and so the final chapter commenced on 17th August 1972, with a note from the Chief Executive

(Railways) to the Chairman of the British Railways Board. In it, the possibly inevitable comment was made that the trains had now reached the stage where "substantial expenditure for overhaul and renovation is required", a figure of £300,000 being quoted for 1973.

The second paragraph of the note contained the damning words, "I have, therefore, agreed that the Pullman trains should be withdrawn from the timetable of 1973, and be replaced by locomotive-hauled, air-conditioned stock", and as if to further justify the decision, the report continued, "Even allowing for some loss of revenue because of the service revisions, which will involve a small reduction in the number of trains, there should be a net benefit over the years 1973 and 1974 of over £350,000". From a loss to a benefit then, compared with the figures quoted in 1969, possibly a different set of

An eight-car set stabled in the carriage sidings at Old Oak Common on 3rd June 1967.
(W Potter/Kidderminster Railway Museum)

standards were being used.

This time there would no reprieve, and no response from the WR is recorded. Paddington was probably just glad that a decision had finally been made. Interestingly, it appears that there was no reference to any public-relations exercise to handle the situation, but with the pending introduction of new air-conditioned stock, the pill would be easier to swallow, anyway.

There then followed an understandable running down of the sets. Maintenance was reduced, and some cannibalisation took place in order to maintain services – indeed from June 1972 onwards there were never five complete sets available, and some considerable swapping of vehicles was undertaken, eventually leaving just three 8-car trains in service for the final months. One of these was a WR 4-car half-set, together with an assortment of former LMR vehicles making up the other four cars.

The first vehicle to be stored was parlour first W60732, which had been taken out of service in June 1972 following complaints over rough riding and associated flats on the wheels. Four months later, in October 1972, Old Oak Common placed former WR power car W60099 in store with a thrown con-rod. There followed a gradual decline, and it is clear that instructions had been given to curtail heavy repairs, indeed cannibalisation of

vehicles was also taking place, as the same instructions had been given to Swindon, where spare engines were simply stored rather than being made ready for use. The previous reference by BRB about the need to spend £300,000 on the trains could now be understood.

The engine situation is interesting, as according to Adrian Curtis, an audit of spares and equipment for the trains in May 1973 revealed that there were three complete spare power units at Swindon, although as mentioned above, they were not ready for use. (It is not known whether this audit was undertaken prior to a possible sale, or whether it was an early move to resurrect the sets, as nearly occurred in September 1973, and as will be described later.) The fact that three spare engines are referred to, together with two (there had originally been three) spare auxiliary power units, is the very first time that concrete figures are given for major spares held for the sets. How ironic that this did not become known until the very end of the trains' lives.

By the end of services in May 1973, just three complete eight car sets remained. One at Old Oak Common (W60094, W60644, W60734, W60744, W60745, W60735, W60645 and W60090), one at Bristol Bath Road (W60098, W60648, W60738, W60748, W60749, W60739, W60649 and W60092), and one at Cardiff

Bristol Bath Road depot open day on 23rd October 1965, and a WR Blue Pullman set is sandwiched between two Hymek diesels. The WR was still justifiably proud of its fleet at this time, and would take every opportunity to promote it to the Press, the public and the enthusiast whenever possible. (*W Potter/Kidderminster Railway Museum*)

(W60096, W60647, W60737, W60747, W60743, W60742, W60731 and W60093).

The other 12 vehicles were also at Old Oak Common, but did not form any complete sets. The one complete set that was there was the one that had been used on the final fast enthusiasts' special and included former LMR power car W60090. The Bath Road set again included a former LMR power car, W60092, and the set at Cardiff was the previously mentioned 8-car train comprising a WR half-set together with four odd vehicles from the LMR (including power car W60093).

The swapping of vehicles within fixed-formation diesel sets was not, of course, uncommon and had been going on for some years within the ordinary DMU fleet. In later years, and indeed up to the present, vehicle swaps amongst HST and other sets are commonplace, but it is more noticeable with different sector and company liveries presenting a "mish-mash" appearance.

The same audit also gives some details of previous repair histories, including the fact that the last major or heavy overhauls had been as far back as July 1967, although in some cases, tyres were being turned at various depots as recently as February 1973. The conclusion reached at the time of the initial approach by the WR over the trains' future in 1969, is that repairs were already be-

ing restricted, and after that date only running maintenance was being carried out.

After withdrawal in May 1973, and with no buyer having been found, it is reasonable to expect that the sets were quickly despatched for scrap, but this is not the case, and indeed a resurrection was considered for a time. Most surprisingly, this was being considered by BR itself, even though they had only recently decided that there was no place for the Pullman trains running in parallel with the new Mark 2 coaching stock.

How this came about is referred to in a memorandum from the Executive Director (Passenger) to the Chief Executive (Railways), at BR Headquarters; it is dated 3rd September 1973. The first sentence reveals everything: "Bearing in mind the difficult situation for Type 4 locomotives likely to arise this winter, I have been considering further the possibility of making use of the Pullman trains now awaiting disposal after displacement from WR services." The "difficult situation" was of the Railway's own doing, as it had had been created by the wholesale withdrawal of various former WR diesel-hydraulic classes. The Warship classes had gone by the end of 1972, considerable inroads had been made into the Hymek class, and the first Westerns were already laid aside.

The note continued with a proposal to reconstitute

Platforms 4 and 5 at Paddington just before 11.00am on 13th March 1968. Two sets are being made ready for service, that to the right for Cardiff, while on the left a former LMR set will later form the Oxford train.

(GP Cooper)

two Pullman sets, augmented to nine cars each in the following formation: Motor-Parlour-Parlour-Kitchen-Parlour-Parlour-Parlour-Parlour-Motor. A projected seating capacity of 294 was given, 204 of which would have been second-class. No further details were given about the vehicles that would have been used, but this would have depended on their condition. This is an interesting parallel to similar ideas that were suggested back in 1966.

The report included an assessment that it would take three months to prepare the trains for their new use, and although no costs were mentioned, necessary "heavy expenditure" would be required. Their intended use was also given, ironically between Paddington and Birmingham, but there is no further elaboration. Two other comments from the note are also interesting; the first was that, if the trains were required for only a limited period of regular use, a smaller amount of work on them might suffice. It was also stated that, "Renovating the sets might then open the way for their use for high quality excursion work, again involving relatively low annual mileage – Scotland for example". All these comments are worthy of further discussion, the three-month timescale in particular. The report is dated September, so if the anticipated motive power situation was due to occur in the coming winter, a three-month timescale to get the sets ready for use would mean that they would not have been available until half way through the winter timetable anyway. The mention of Scotland and tourist work is a pleasing and perhaps underestimated idea, we will never know just how popular this type of Pullman tour might have been.

Despite the proposal being an unlikely possibility, further correspondence on the topic does exist. This is dated 20th September, and expands slightly on the earlier note, referring this time to the creation of four sets, each of nine vehicles, two to be ready in January/February 1974 and the remaining two in March. This time, a cost of £200,000 is quoted, (a figure that was obtained, it was stated, verbally from BREL) although it was acknowledged that costs would rise due to, "vandalism and ageing of equipment" while in storage. It was also suggested that one of the four should be kept as a spare.

Clearly, there was other paperwork (not yet located), as there is mention of the preparation of timings over the proposed route. There is also an acknowledgement that the sets in a 2+7 formation would be likely to be poor timekeepers. Elsewhere, there is mention of difficulties with the sets not being cleared to run into Birmingham New Street. It was as though some factions were already against a resurrection, perhaps hardly surprising, with difficulties being accentuated rather than there being a will to succeed.

This is borne out in a reference to the renovation of the sets, and where it should take place. "Presumably BREL would carry out the work at Swindon, which has traditionally dealt with them, although I must point out that this will certainly pose industrial relations problems due to the agreed run-down of facilities at that works." Swindon finally closed in 1985, but it is clear that the decision had been taken at least twelve years prior to this. It

was also noted that while servicing could be carried out at the Pullman shed at Old Oak Common, this very facility was shortly to be used for maintaining the prototype HST set, and it was considered that, "there would certainly be a risk to running both forms of traction which I would not be prepared to take". This last comment is difficult to comprehend, and can only be seen as another obstruction to the re-introduction of the trains.

Finally, what of the comment about running the sets between Paddington and Birmingham? Were the principal services on this route not concentrated on Euston, the former WR line via High Wycombe having been reduced to a secondary service? What also of the possible involvement of the LMR? None of these issues was addressed in any of the papers.

In the event, of course, none of this is relevant as, for whatever reason (and it appears from later notes that the industrial relations situation was the main sticking point), the trains were not reintroduced. Instead, they remained in store, suffering from the ageing and vandalism that had been referred to, until eventually, scrapping was the only option.

By this time, space constraints resulted in the vehicles being concentrated at Swindon, Old Oak Common, and Bristol St Phillips Marsh. Additionally this was the period of the infamous power-cuts associated with industrial disputes and the "three day week" and accordingly, certain redundant power and auxiliary power cars were stationed at Bristol Bath Road, Bristol Temple Meads and Cardiff to act as emergency generators. Those at Bristol Bath Road were W60093 and W60731, whilst stabled at Platform 4 of the neighbouring Bristol Temple Meads station were W60096 and W60647. Cardiff had W60648/9, although it is not clear if these were located at Canton depot or the station itself. Whether any, or all, were used for their intended purpose during the dispute or even if substitutions also took place involving those referred to is not certain. Probably the last to be finally moved were W60096 and W60647 from Bristol Temple Meads in July 1974.

Even at the last minute, there was still a glimmer of salvation. At least one 8-car set was still intact at Swindon at the start of 1974 – was it possible that it had been transferred there to be refurbished? Apparently, it was less affected by deterioration than the others. It was also the subject of a widely reported preservation attempt that was covered in the *Railway Magazine* at the time:

"Ten Blue Pullman carriages, withdrawn from service by the Western Region in May 1973, have been saved from scrap by a private group with the principle intention of making a train of six or more of them available for charter over British Railways. They comprise the first two (and the last surviving) of the diesel-electric motor brake firsts Nos W60090/1, two kitchen firsts M60731/3, and six parlour seconds W60644-9. All are to be towed to BRE Glasgow workshops for complete renovation and repainting in the 'Nanking blue' livery carried when they were supplied by Metropolitan-Cammell in 1960. Because the number of drivers experienced in their

This is a former LMR 6-car unit, still retaining its original livery, but operating on the WR – possibly on the short-lived Paddington to Oxford service. While an excellent idea, it is a pity that no consideration appears to have been given to a regular peak-hour service from Worcester or even Hereford. (*RHG Simpson*)

operation is limited, initially operations will be limited to the WR, probably from sidings rented from BR, but they could eventually be accommodated at a preservation centre when not on main line charter work. To assist in maintenance, the Blue Pullman Group is seeking official drawings, circuit diagrams, running manuals and so forth, which might now be in the hands of collectors."

It should be remembered that this was a period when the private use of steam locomotives on BR was banned and it would be many years before a privately owned diesel would be permitted.

At such a recent point in the Blue Pullman story, it might be expected that information on the preservation attempt would be easy to locate, but the reverse is the case. No details have come to light about the preservationists referred to in the *Railway Magazine*, nor how close they might have come to achieving their aim.

Thought was also given to a set (or part of one) being used by Rolls Royce as a "rolling test bed" in connection with the APT Gas Turbine experiments, but this was not pursued either.

It appears that the remaining vehicles were simply concentrated at Swindon or at Ninian Park sidings, Cardiff, and the possibility that they contained blue asbestos, would have made their disposal a protracted affair. Discussions about the eventual fate of the vehicles dragged on for some time, and for as long as some vehicles remained, there was conjecture over their possible sale or preservation.

Eventually all were sold to Birds of Morriston, near Swansea, for scrapping, although it is believed that some found their way to Messrs TW Ward at Briton Ferry and G Cohen at Swansea. The suggested asbestos content led to the vehicles being impounded at Ninian Park for a while, and soil contaminated by asbestos was subsequently found at both Morriston and Briton Ferry, leading, it was stated, to considerable repercussions later on although further information on this is not available.

So, was the Blue Pullman story one that ended with the premature withdrawal of the trains, or were they really life-expired, given that when they were introduced it was predicted that they would go through to 1990? Was the whole Blue Pullman escapade actually just a poor business decision?

An independent assessment is really not possible, unless it is based purely on personal opinion. There are several issues to consider, and so it is necessary to refer back briefly to some of the topics discussed previously.

On balance, BR was right to attempt to capture the luxury market, but whether using luxury trains with very limited use was the right approach is not so clear-cut. The difficulty in drawing conclusions 30 years after the demise of the sets, and almost half a century since they were conceived, is that opinions are based on the standards of today.

With hindsight, the best solution at the time would

have been to improve a number of front-line services on all lines, but in reality this was just not possible. Hampered, as they were, by many years of under-investment (a familiar situation some fifty years later), the luxury train concept would inevitably be restricted, simply because it was required to operate amongst other services on existing tracks, competing with them for space, and taking their share of delays.

However, without realising it, BR and the Blue Pullman trains had shown that the concept of a fixed-formation train was a well-balanced approach, especially at a time when costs were rising and all means had to be found to reduce them. The ability to dispense with shunting movements, resulting in quicker turnaround times (exemplified when a spare or replacement set was needed in a hurry) was a factor that was very much in the trains' favour.

It is appropriate therefore to explore the fixed-formation idea further. As far as the LMR is concerned, it is worth looking at something that happened on 13th January 1961. It was reported that the up Midland Pullman had rapidly lost power near Bedford (the reason is not known, but it is possible that one of the power cars failed) resulting in an arrival nine minutes late at St Pancras. It was now after midday, and the return service was due to leave St Pancras again just six hours later, meanwhile, the spare set was at Reddish near Manchester, over 180 miles distant, and yet it was immediately sent for. It worked south, and arrived in time to be restocked ready to take up the booked return working.

The Western Region could also rise to the occasion when required, such as at Paddington on 9th February 1962, when the 10.10am Bristol Pullman departure failed after travelling no more than a few yards along the platform. Within just 25 minutes, passengers had been transferred to a diesel Pullman set that had arrived from Swansea, which then managed to regain a further five minutes (net) to Birmingham, despite suffering some severe checks due to difficulties with preceding trains and temporary speed restrictions.

The other advantage in favour of the fixed formation was its predictable performance. The percentage increase in weight between a part load and a full load was negligible when plotting timetable paths, and compared favourably with the loading variations that applied to the locomotive-hauled services of the period.

Having described best practice, it is only fair to refer to the opposite as well. The 11th April 1963 was a bad day for the WR, as all three of its diesel Pullman sets were out of action for various reasons, resulting in loco haulage of various "scratch" standby sets. Arguably, even worse, was the situation that beset Paddington on 1st December 1960. On this occasion, the 10.10am Bristol Pullman service consisted of nothing better than ordinary coaching stock that had previously arrived as the 9.38am from Henley-in-Arden. Castle class 4-6-0 5043 "Earl of Mount Edgcumbe" was put in charge, and for unknown reasons, managed to lose a further 20 minutes westwards on top of its 10-minute late departure. (The earlier com-

ment about steam never having been used as a substitute for the Blue Pullmans still applies, as this was on ordinary coaching stock.)

Finally, it should be said that the Midland lines were not devoid of difficulties either as, on 21st December 1960, the down service from St Pancras was formed of six ordinary coaches and a Peak class diesel! The WR was perhaps more likely to suffer failures as their three sets were used far more intensely. The temptation is to look back at the Pullman sets with revered admiration, but they were certainly not perfect.

Without doubt, the jewel in the crown as far as the WR was concerned, was the service to Birmingham, and Paddington seemed oblivious to any sensible planning when it came to introducing the new trains to and from Bristol in 1960. The new 110-minute Pullman service, on which a supplementary fare was charged, was a whole ten minutes slower than the erstwhile Bristolian. It is true that fears over the behaviour of the Warship class diesels heading the Bristolian later led to the service being slowed to 105 minutes, but pre-service trials had shown that the Pullman sets were easily capable of an 87-minute schedule. Add, say, eight minutes recovery time, and the result would have been a very attractive 95 minutes - better than the Bristolian by five minutes.

Both the fast services were routed via Badminton rather than Bath, but the WR scored another own goal by setting the evening departure time for the Bristol service from Paddington in a path used by a fast service that a number of influential Bath commuters patronised. These travellers were vociferous in their complaints that their return from London now involved a journey time extended by no less than 40 minutes, in addition to a change of trains. The result was that, just over six weeks after the Pullman service began (from 17th October to be precise), it was rerouted via Bath, and a stop at that location was added. The fact that the printed public timetable had to be heavily revised mid-way through its currency was not helped by at least three other unconnected services also having to be retimed for varying reasons. Perhaps Paddington had the last laugh, however, as they could now charge those same Bath commuters a supplement to travel home!

The Bath route was now the preferred choice for the diesel Pullman services, and moving ahead in time, it should be mentioned that the Bristol Pullman service was accelerated in 1968 to 100 minutes inclusive of the stop at Bath. The train was revised to 105 minutes for its last months of operation from 1972, but this was due to an additional stop at Chippenham.

Clearly, Paddington had learnt a harsh lesson, and they were determined that mistakes would not to be repeated with the introduction South Wales Pullman. Trials had shown that it was possible to shave no less than 35 minutes from the schedule of the steam-hauled South Wales Pullman, which dated from 27th June 1955. (The steam service had commenced two weeks later than intended, due to an ASLEF strike at the time.) The diesel Pullman meant that Swansea was now a minimum of 3hr

35min from Paddington.

Having dealt with the services, what about the trains themselves, and in particular the ride quality? Were they really as bad as has been made out? The same type of bogie had been used extensively on the continent including under vehicles operating the prestige SNCF Mistral express in France. It has been suggested that even before the Pullmans ran, trials of the new bogies under Mark 1 stock did reveal some deficiencies, but this was possibly accentuated by the generally shorter length of British coaches compared with their European counterparts, together with the weight of extra equipment carried by the home-grown product. Some of the Pullman vehicles were certainly in this category, while others appeared to ride better than their neighbours. Generally the trailers were the most acceptable of all.

This situation with the bogies is really quite surprising, and would appear to indicate that a totally new bogie was tested, found not to be completely suitable, and yet was still used under the new trains! Without implying blame or criticism of either BR or the manufacturer, the later riding problems must surely have been foreseen. No doubt the trials, and the subsequent decision to use an unsuitable product, generated an inordinate amount of correspondence, but none has been located. Was the design of the new trains simply too advanced technically? (Remember, the order was placed with Metropolitan-Cammell in December 1956.)

If so, and without any evidence to support or refute these beliefs, what follows is a painful but true comparison. Less than a decade earlier, the Southern Railway, and its successor the Southern Region under Bulleid, had persisted in the use of sleeve valves in the design of the "Leader" locomotive, even when experiments with a "Brighton" Atlantic had proved them to be less than ideal. The situations appear identical; in both cases tests were carried out which showed up the deficiencies, and yet even while the tests were being undertaken, the intended design on which the item was to be used was still being proceeded with, without any major modification.

In reality, the Swiss bogie just did not suit British trackwork. The WR sets, while poor at times, did not attract as much criticism, and this was for two reasons. First, there were more lightweight trailer vehicles per train, and second (although this will not necessarily be appreciated by devotees of the LMR) the standard of track maintenance on the WR was better than out of St. Pancras. (It was not much better out of Euston either in later years, but this was as a result of the punishing behaviour of some of the AC electric locomotives with their nose-suspended traction motors.) It is not for nothing that the main line out of Paddington is known as "Brunel's billiard table" even today! At the risk of upsetting the Western diehard, however, it should also be noted that the East Coast main line out of Kings Cross was even better, and to complete the picture, the least said about certain examples of Southern trackwork, the better!

As a partial defence, the tests with the Metro-

Schlieren bogie might not have been intended to verify their suitability for the Pullman services. At the time, BR was seeking a new bogie design for its main-line corridor stock. The final result was the B4 type, but an interim solution was the heavy "Commonwealth" bogie, which because of its weight, was also expensive. Had the Swiss bogie come up to expectations, it might have been adopted as standard. Latterly, the BR double-bolster bogie gave a better ride at 90mph than did the Pullman bogie at a lower speeds, while by the end of the 1960s, the BR Mark 2D coaches, with the B4 bogie, were giving passengers a far better ride, to faster schedules, and without the necessity to pay a supplement.

The Pullman sets also lost out due to their limited utilisation when first built. This could easily have been overcome if more had been built, but it must have been obvious that, in the cost-conscious 1960s, there was no way the railway could sanction a spare train set almost permanently held in reserve.

Accordingly, full utilisation was required, but how was this to be achieved? Had the two sets remained on the Midland, perhaps Liverpool would have been the next logical destination. Electrification, however, meant that on the LMR, the trains would be redundant, and it made sense to concentrate all the units in one place, where staff were familiar with them.

The Blue Pullman services might perhaps be remembered as a useful "stop-gap", and one that saved an amount of business for the railway in the interim between the steam age and the age of electrification and the HSTs. On balance, BR was probably correct in believing (for a while, at least) that the appearance of the diesel Pullmans alone was enough to justify a slower schedule.

But by the late 1960s, it was only a matter of time before someone decided, "enough was enough". A warning of this came as early as 1969, when all the mid-day fill-in turns disappeared, and the sets were nowhere near as smart and neat as they had once been. This was partly a change of fashion, but in the opinion of many, the corporate livery did nothing to help. Blue and white was far more preferable to white and blue, and perhaps the biggest error BR made was this livery change. White and blue changed the appearance of the sets overnight from something special to something dowdy and aged.

The Blue Pullman concept showed the way, and was never intended to be an experiment – more a prototype. They were not alone at having an early demise either, as proved by some of the contemporary Inter-City diesel sets. The HST from the mid-1970s would be the next big step forward, and was the most successful move away from the conventional locomotive and coaches. In the opinion of many, the HST was the saviour of the railway system, for without it, Serpell and his contemporaries might have had their way. (The Serpell Report proposed the wholesale closure of almost the whole railway network, save for a section of the East Coast main line.) It is a matter of regret that as the 21st century continues, the same timetabling difficulties that beset the operation of the diesel Pullman services still affect services today. This is despite cutbacks to local services over the years and the closure of wayside stations and uneconomic branch lines, all of which (allied to modern signalling) should have reduced line congestion. It is surely ironic that despite all this, the railways generally seem ever more incapable of delivering a reliable service.

The final verdict was delivered by both General Sir Brian Robertson (Chairman of the BTC) and Dr Beeching, both of whom independently expressed their approval of the use of luxury train sets for business travel. This is a particularly remarkable statement from Dr Beeching, given his preference for standardised travel, with no peaks in traffic and no special workings.

The Blue Pullman style of train (not necessarily exactly as the original design) was intended to woo the business traveller, with the intention of similar trains being introduced on other routes to create a pool of similar vehicles. This did, of course, happen later - not for the business traveller, but for the masses, in the form of the HST. (The approval of the luxury train concept by Dr Beeching is perhaps the most difficult to reconcile, as he is on record as disapproving of anything different from the regular service, as shown by his well-documented attempts to dampen peaks in holiday and seasonal traffic. However, in 1963, he spoke on behalf of the BRB to the effect that future plans for an extension of the Pullman network had been predicted, although no plans for the actual construction of the trains had yet been prepared.)

The relentless march of technology and innovation throughout the 1960s meant that finding suitable work for the Blue Pullman sets was becoming more difficult every day. It cannot be said, either, that BR did not make all reasonable efforts to find gainful employment for the sets. The story that, at sometime in the middle of the night, one or more sets were spirited away to a secret store in rural England or Wales is nothing but a myth. Physically, the demise of the trains might have taken place around 1974, but it had really begun at least five years earlier. The trains, with their unique Nanking blue livery, have now been consigned to history for far longer than they actually existed. Their lifetime was short, their peak years even shorter, and their usefulness is likely to be debated for years to come.

Withdrawn power cars and vehicles at Old Oak Common on 3rd November 1973. Identification is unfortunately not possible, but it is likely that the one nearest the camera is 60091.   (*Antony M Ford Collection*)

APPENDIX A

Vehicle Numbering, Original Set Formations, and the "Wells Fargo" Sets

LMR Sets

On the LMR in 1960, the sets were referred to as "Train 1" and "Train 2". These were made up of the following vehicles:

Train 1: 60091, 60731, 60741, 60740, 60730, 60090
Train 2: 60092, 60732, 60742, 60743, 60733, 60093

The vehicles operating on the LMR all had their running numbers prefixed with the letter M. The set formation was as follows:

Motor Car, Kitchen Car, Parlour Car, Parlour Car, Kitchen Car, Motor Car.
Total seating: 132 first class passengers.

WR Sets

It is not thought that the WR sets were designated with "train" numbering. The set formation was as follows:
Motor Car, Parlour Car, Kitchen Car, Parlour Car, Parlour Car, Kitchen Car, Parlour Car, Motor Car.
Total seating: 218 (98 first class and 120 second class).

Vehicle Dimensions

- DMB (Driving Motor Brake): 66ft 5 ½in x 9ft 3in
- All other vehicles: 65ft 6in

- DMBF (Driving Motor Brake First) and DMBS (Driving Motor Brake Second): 67ton 10cwt
- Non-driving MPSL and MKFL: 45ton 10cwt
- All other vehicles: 33 tons

When new, the wheel diameter was 3ft 6in, reducing to a minimum 3ft 3 ½in when worn.

The WR estimate for the weight of an 8-car set half stocked (tare) was 335.86 tons. When in full working order with all seats filled and including luggage, the weight was 357.38tons. The total length was 545ft 1in.

Bogies

An accurate assessment of the bogie weights is given in a diagram accompanying the WR Test Run of 16th June 1960 (see Page 35), which refers to the following bogie weights:

- DMBS: leading 33.8ton, trailing 30.2ton
- MPSL: powered 25.15ton, un-powered 17.12ton
- TKFL: 16.82ton (kitchen end) and 15.42ton
- TPFL: both 14.71ton

The vehicles had either a "heavy" or "light" bogie, which could be either 9ft 6in or 8ft 6in wheelbase. As originally equipped the leading bogies were 9ft 6in as were also all the powered bogies. Trailing bogies were always 8ft 6in wheelbase.

An 8-car WR set had the following bogie sequence:
LB, MB(H), MB(L), TB(H), TB(H), TB(L), TB(L), TB (L) (followed by the same in reverse order for the second half set).

Build Details

For administrative purposes the vehicles were also each allotted a schedule number by the Pullman Car Co in the series 355-390. This number was not actually shown on the vehicle.

Type	Number	Class	Lot
DMBFL	60090 to 60093	251/1	30553
DMBS	60094 to 60099	251/2	30554
MPSL	60644 to 60649	261/1	30555
MKFL	60730 to 60733	261/1	30556
TKFL	60734 to 60739	261/2	30557
TPFL	60740 to 60749	261/2	30557

Formation of Spare Train Sets (the "Wells Fargo" Sets)

According to RW Kidner, the first formed spare set for the WR was used between 26th February 1962 and 12th March 1962. The formation witnessed on 26th August 1964, deputising for the Birmingham Pullman, was 54, 106, 340, 352, 344, 105, and 55.

It is believed this set was replaced later by a rake of conventional Pullman vehicles, which were then all designated 2nd class by the Pullman Car Co. This was objected to by passengers and accordingly some cosmetic changes in numberings and the additions of names were made.

Car	Pullman Register	Name	Type
66	188	Avon	Parlour
73	226	Ceteia	Parlour
105	210	Hebe	Kitchen
74	227	Melandra	Parlour
60	215	Severn	Kitchen
106	211	Thalia	Kitchen
61	216	Thames	Kitchen
109	212	Thetis	Kitchen
35	193	Wye	Parlour

Possibly posed for publicity purposes, this is an unidentified 8-car set outside the, then new, Tyseley diesel depot at Birmingham in 1962. While they were, no doubt, occasional visitors to Tyseley, general maintenance of the sets on the WR was concentrated on Old Oak Common. *(CP Boocock)*

A Bristol Pullman set passes through Newbury in 1966. The photographer recalls that he had just parked the car after returning from a commercial job with his 5in x 4in Micro Press camera, and was walking back to his studio when he saw it coming. How he got the plate in, and the camera focused, he doesn't know! *(DE Canning)*

Extract from the British Railways Midland Region Magazine, November 1960

Quickest, quietest... that's the Midland Pullman

Says Miles Wyvern

When you board the Midland Pullman at Manchester Central, as I did the other day, the first impression you get is one of luxury and soundlessness. Once through the mirror-finished vestibule doors, the familiar station noises are cut off with disconcerting suddenness. You're in a warm air-conditioned world of foot-hugging carpets, clean table-linen and inviting upholstery. Even the conversation of nearby passengers comes through as a mere murmur, so well are the internal acoustics arranged.

A smart attendant showed me to my seat, seizing hat and coat and placing them quickly on the rack - presumably lest I should attempt, unpardonably, to do that little chore myself. Since most of my fellow passengers were displaying an air of *sang-froid,* which apparently bespoke a lifetime of travelling on such a train, I stifled my interest and curiosity with a similar cloak of sophistication. Settling down in the armchair seat and promising myself a session with the two intriguing seat adjustment controls later in the journey, I opened that morning's *Guardian* and attempted to read.

A smooth start

It says much for that newspaper that, surrounded by so much to distract my interest, I eventually became absorbed. When a few minutes later I looked at my watch it showed 8.51. Good heavens! A minute past departure time and we hadn't moved. . .correction, we hadn't *apparently* moved. A look through the windows showed the soundless outside world rolling by. We had actually pulled out of the station without the slightest sensation of movement.

I was able to check the smooth starting of the train after its single intermediate stop at Cheadle Heath, where several more passengers joined the train. The departure was a beauty - and spoke well for the draw and buff gear between the coaches, which was specially designed to assist in smooth pick-up of speed by the train when starting.

Even as we gathered speed there was no increase in noise, no vibration. It was uncanny. Like travelling in a vacuum. Fifty miles an hour felt like five on this train. Trains going the other way glided past the window like ghosts, quickly, silently. The clickety-clack of the rail joints was all but inaudible even in tunnels.

As we slipped steadily along at 70-80 mph leaving Manchester far astern and entering the beautiful mist-shrouded Peak District, it struck me that one of the effects of quietness and comfort inside the train was that passengers tended to take a much greater interest in the passing scenery. They stared with fascination as the views from the windows changed abruptly when the train emerged from cuttings and tunnels. It was all rather like watching a silent film in glorious colour.

Attracting attention

The windows are double-glazed, so there is no misting, and no penetration by outside noise. In sunny weather Venetian blinds can be lowered and adjusted between the two panes of glass. If you have ever had the luck to travel in a really swish Rolls Royce you will have an idea of what it is like on the Midland Pullman – not only because of the comfort but in the stares you attract from passers-by. For the blue and cream streamliner gets a good looking over from everyone *en route* – railwaymen, passengers at stations, farm workers and all manner of trackside rubbernecks. There was even one man, oddly enough in his shirtsleeves despite the chilly morning, who grimly shot us with his ciné camera from a perch on the trackside fence near Harpenden. One imagined that he had rushed from his house in mid-shave and then dashed across the damp fields to be in time to record our passing.

Motorway crawlers

One point in the journey where the sensation of speed intruded for a moment was near Luton where the M1 motorway runs parallel to the line for a mile or so. Cars which must have been travelling in the sixties appeared to be crawling as we swiftly overtook them.

While it is difficult to analyse the feeling of well-being experienced as a passenger on this train, it is without any doubt due in large measure to the solicitousness of the train staff. The service is really superb. Meals and drinks are served quickly and quietly with calm efficiency. The Pullman attendants – former London Midland dining car men, do a grand job. The Conductor was Maurice Walton, 36 years on the railway, who used to work on the Marylebone – Manchester run. It was he who announced over the train's public address system that tickets were to be collected and, later, that the train was approaching destination. If there had been any delay he could have kept passengers in the picture.

"But it doesn't do to use the p.a. system too much," he told me. "Our passengers wouldn't appreciate such intrusion. I use it only when I think it will be of help to them."

The best in Europe

We drew into St Pancras on time feeling like VIPs. For me it was a memorable trip, a glimpse into the future of railway travel. For even though it will be a long time before all main line trains are like the Midland Pullman, this does represent the ultimate aim.

The six-coach train conveys 132 first class passengers and loadings on the Manchester – London journeys have been good, and are increasing. It received much favourable Press publicity when it came into service on 4 July last and its reception among businessmen has been outstandingly good. The Midland Pullman made a great impression on a team of eight American railway executives who recently visited Britain and six continental countries. They called it: "The best train in Europe".

APPENDIX C

Working Instructions

British Railways (Western Region) Circular no 544

Working of Diesel Pullman trains

To come into operation 12th September 1960

The following instructions will apply in connection with the working of Diesel Pullman Trains on the Western Region:-

These trains are fitted with three-tone warning horns at each end. The three tones must always be sounded when it is necessary to give a warning. For standard or local whistle code purposes the lower note only must be used.

All concerned must warn men employed under their supervision who may be required to work on the permanent way or to walk upon or cross running lines, of the importance of observing the warning and that they must be prepared for the trains to approach quietly and at high speed. Upon hearing the warning, the Driver should be given an acknowledgment whenever possible. It is important that men engaged on permanent way work etc., shall move promptly to a point of safety upon sighting or receiving audible warning of the approach of a train. If it is necessary for Diesel Pullman trains to work over a section of line where they are not normally scheduled to run, Drivers of such trains must sound the three-tone warning horn in accordance with Rule 127 and when approaching curves, level crossings, barrow crossings, overbridges, Gangers huts and other buildings adjacent to the line upon which the trains are running. In such cases prior advice must, where possible, be issued to all concerned, particularly permanent way staff, by means of printed or other notice. In emergency, when it is not possible to issue prior notice, the Drivers of such diesel trains must be advised.

The speed of trains must not exceed 10 mph when proceeding along carriage or repair sidings, or sidings in Motive Power Depots. Before entering sheds, Drivers must bring their trains to a stand and give a warning signal on the horn to staff who may be at work inside. The speed of trains inside a shed must not exceed 5 mph.

STATION STOPS

In all cases, owing to the use of a standard formation, the trains should come to rest at the same position every day and this will enable the station staff to assist passengers in taking up a position as near as possible to the entrance of the coach in which their seats have been reserved. Station stops and turn-round times have been kept to a minimum consistent with the duties to be carried out and it is essential, therefore, that station staff and train crews should do all they can to avoid delays.

The following stopping points have been laid down:-
BATH SPA At the 9-car station stop signs on both Up and Down platforms.
BRISTOL (T.M.) Platform 9, at the point opposite the white ring indicated on platform support pillar opposite the Chief Inspector's Office. Other platforms at the normal stopping point for main line trains.
LEAMINGTON SPA At the 8-car station stop signs on both Up and Down platforms.
SOLIHULL At the 8-car station stop signs on both Up and Down platforms.
BIRMINGHAM (S.H.) At the 8-car station stop signs on both Up and Down platforms.
WOLVERHAMPTON (L.L.) At the 8-car station stop signs on both Up and Down platforms.

1. WORKING INSTRUCTIONS

1. The Rules and Regulations are applicable to Diesel Pullman trains except as modified below:-
(i) Rules:-
127. Each driving compartment is equipped with a sealed detonator case with a red flag. The Driver, when taking over, must ensure the seal is intact. The Driver must have with him in the driving compartment a handlamp with red shade.
141. The Guard's signal to start the train will be given in accordance with the bell code shewn in Instruction No. 6.
(ii) Brake Regulations.
Diesel Pullman Trains operate on the Westinghouse Electro-Pneumatic compressed air brake.
The following Regulations will apply: Reg. 1 – Description – The normal brake pressure is 70lbs. per square inch and is indicated in the Guard's Brake Vans and Driving Cabs.
Reg. 297 Before starting from Depot etc. The Driver must advise the Guard when he is ready to make the brake test with him from the rear Guard's compartment; the Guard must check that:-
(a) The brake pipe is charged to 70lbs. per square inch.
(b) On opening the Guard's valve and reducing the brake pipe pressure to zero, check with the Driver that the brake cylinder pressure rises to at least 45 lbs. per square inch.
(c) Must return the Guard's valve handle to the closed position and see that the brake pipe pressure is restored to 70lbs. per square inch.
The arrangements for conducting the test will be carried out on the Loudaphone equipment.
This test must be made daily before the train is taken into service.
The Guard will be held responsible for satisfying himself the brake has been tested in accordance with these instructions and is continuous throughout the train.

APPENDIX

2. HEAD CODES.

Electric head lamps exhibiting the standard Class "A" or "C" head code will be carried.

3. AUTOMATIC WARNING SYSTEM ON DIESEL PULLMAN TRAINS.

The Apparatus in the Train, which is air braked, varies from that for vacuum braked trains as previously described, although the audible signals are again produced by a bell for the "all clear" aspect and a siren for the "caution" aspect. The operation of the contact shoe is also similar on air and vacuum braked vehicles.

The cab apparatus is placed behind the driver on the bulkhead with the handle of a Sealed Isolating Cock projecting slightly from the face of the enclosing cabinet. The associated Timing Reservoir and Application Valve are situated in close proximity below the cab floor. The A.W.S. Power Governor is fixed beside the A.W.S. Battery Box on the other side of the bulkhead. A Reset button is situated on the Driver's desk and above it is an A.W.S. IN/OUT of USE Switch and an A.W.S. IN/OUT of USE Indicator.

The shoe switch is connected with an electrically controlled valve in such a way that whenever this valve is opened, air will be released through the siren from the brake pipe thus sounding the siren.

This occurs when a train passes over a "dead" ramp, associated with a Distant signal showing a "caution" aspect resulting in the brakes being fully applied together with a cutting off of the power to the traction motors and the diesel engines reverting to idling, and this will happen within three seconds of the siren first sounding if suitable action is not taken in the manner described hereafter.

The Driver, by depressing and releasing the Reset button within the 3 second warning period, can acknowledge the warning given by the siren, stopping the siren sounding and avoiding the brake application and cutting off of traction power.

If the caution signal is not acknowledged as described above within the 3 seconds warning period, the ensuing brake application can only be cancelled by first returning the power control handle to the Notch 0 position and then depressing and releasing the Reset button. The traction power, which was cut simultaneously with the brake application, can only be reapplied when the brakes have become fully released.

When the train passes over an electrified ramp, which is associated with a signal displaying the "all clear" aspect, the bell will ring.

The Reset button cannot be used to forestall the sounding of the siren. If the Reset button is depressed at any other time than after receiving the caution warning from a "dead" ramp the siren will sound and, if held depressed for more than 3 seconds, the effect will be the same as for an uncancelled warning.

If the train is proceeding very slowly over an unelectrified ramp, or is standing on an unelectrified ramp, the siren will sound, but the full brake application and cutting off of the traction power can be avoided by the Driver holding down the Reset button, which will stop the siren sounding. When the shoe clears the ramp the siren will sound again and the Reset button must then be quickly released if the Driver wishes to regain full control of the train.

When the Driver takes charge of a train, before moving the train he must observe the following rules:-
Non-driving Cab.
(a) The Main battery isolating switch must be "IN".
(b) Check that the A.W.S. isolating cock is sealed.
(c) The A.W.S. IN/OUT of USE switch must be in the OUT of USE position, and the Indicator must read A.W.S. OUT of USE.
Driving Cab.
(a) The main locomotive battery switch must be "IN".
(b) Check that the A.W.S. isolating cock is sealed.
(c) The A.W.S. IN/OUT of USE switch must be in the IN USE position and the Indicator must read A.W.S. IN USE.
(d) The A.W.S. apparatus must be reset by depressing and releasing the Reset Button.

If the A.W.S. is not switched into use the siren will sound after the Forward/Reverse handle is moved from the "OFF" position, until the A.W.S. is engaged as above.

After resetting the A.W.S. or when recharging the brake pipe from a low brake pipe pressure, with the A.W.S. reset, the Application Valve will vent to atmosphere for a short period of time until its reservoir is charged sufficiently to reseat it.

The working of the A.W.S. equipment on the train must be tested before the train is moved from its stabling point and at any other time as may be deemed necessary.

The following procedure must be carried out in each driving cab:- Depress Deadman's Pedal and select direction (Forward or Reverse).

Allow A.W.S. siren to sound and after 3 seconds delay note that the Brake Pipe Pressure falls at least 30lbs. p.s.i. and the Brake Cylinder Pressure rises to at least 45lbs. p.s.i.

Place A.W.S. IN/OUT of USE switch to the A.W.S. IN USE position when A.W.S. Indicator must show IN USE and reset by depressing and releasing Reset Button. After a short delay the Brake Cylinder Pressure will fall to zero and the Brake Pipe pressure will rise to 70lbs. p.s.i.

When the Driver leaves the Driving Cab, the following procedure must be observed:- The A.W.S. IN/OUT of USE switch must be placed in the OUT of USE position when the IN/OUT of USE Indicator must read A.W.S. OUT of USE.

If the A.W.S. IN/OUT of USE switch is moved to the OUT of USE position before the Forward/Reverse handle is moved to the "OFF" position the siren will sound between the two movements.

Any irregularities must be dealt with as described under Section IV (a) Clause 7 of the Regional Appendix.

154

If it is not possible to reset the A.W.S. due to a failure of any part of the A.W.S. equipment on the train, the A.W.S. must be isolated by breaking the seal and turning the handle of the Isolating Cock. Movement of this cock to the Isolated position causes the IN/OUT of USE Indicator to read A.W.S. OUT of USE Irrespective of the position of the IN/OUT of USE switch. Breaking of the seal and use of the Isolating Cock must be reported.

4. LOUDAPHONE COMMUNICATION.

The Loudaphone apparatus is a means by which the Driver and Guard may speak to each other, or exchange bell signals but it does not in any way relieve staff from their obligation to carry out the relevant Rules and Regulations.

A buzzer, which is actuated by the depression of the "call" button on the loudaphone, or the signal push above Van doors, is provided in both the Guard's and Driver's compartments and this communication must always be used for the exchange of signals in accordance with the standard code shown in the Instructions for Working Multiple-Unit Mechanical Diesel Trains. An additional signal push which will operate the buzzer in the Driver's cab is provided over the door of each Guard's compartment.

Standard bell codes will be used for all normal movements but the Driver, if requiring to speak to the Guard, or the Guard, if requiring to speak to the Driver, must send on the call button the code 3 pause 3 "Guard required to speak to Driver," or "Driver required to speak to Guard," and the man at the other end must acknowledge by repetition as detailed in the Instructions referred to above. Conversation may then proceed provided both men keep the "Speak" button depressed.

The apparatus must only be used for essential conversations on matters affecting the working of the train and, except in the case of emergency, should not be used when the train is in motion. The apparatus may also be used by Shunters, in the absence of Guards, in order to communicate with Drivers in connection with shunting operations.

In order to avoid any possibility of unauthorised use of the apparatus in Driver's cabs the door between the generator compartments and the Guard's compartment and the exterior door of the Driver's compartment must be kept locked when the Driver's cab is not in use.

5. DIESEL PULLMAN TRAINS MUST NOT CONVEY TAIL TRAFFIC.

6. COMMUNICATION BETWEEN GUARD AND DRIVER

The following code of bell signals between Guard and Driver must always be used by means of the bell communication provided:-

1.   Stop
2.   Start
3.   Set-back
3-3.   Guard required by Driver
         Guard or Driver attend telephone (where provided)
4.   Slow down when propelling.
5.   Driver or Guard leaving train in accordance with rules.
6.   Draw up.

These bell codes must be acknowledged by repetition.
In cases of failure of the bell communication, hand signals must be used except as indicated in the second paragraph of Instruction No. 10.

7. PROPELLING

Except during shunting operations, propelling must only be resorted to where specially authorised.

When propelling, a speed of 5 m.p.h. must not be exceeded and the Guard or Shunter must ride in the leading driving cab, keep a good look-out, operate the warning horn when necessary, and be prepared to stop the train as required by application of the emergency brake. The Guard or Shunter must carefully observe all signals and signal to the Driver as may be necessary in accordance with the bell codes shown in Instruction No. 6. In the event of failure of the bell communication the train must be driven from the leading end.

Trains must be driven from the leading end when proceeding on to another train or entering Carriage or Repair Sheds.

8. FIRE PRECAUTIONS

In the event of an engine becoming overheated, a small red light will be exhibited on the solebar on the side of the vehicle concerned. Should this red light be observed by a Signalman, he must endeavour to bring the train to a stand but if the train enters the section ahead the provisions of Block Regulation 17- "Stop and Examine Train" must be carried out.

Each driving cab is equipped with two hand operated fire extinguishers of the CO_2 gas type; each Guard's compartment and each trailer is provided with one two-gallon CO_2 water type hand operated extinguisher. In addition, automatic fire extinguishing apparatus is fitted on the underframe of motor vehicles. In the event or a fire developing in one of the engines, the extinguishing equipment will come into operation and at the same time ring a bell in the Driver's compartment. After the train has been stopped in accordance with Rule 188, the Driver must proceed to the affected engine and take with him a fire extinguisher and, in the case of trains conveying passengers, must carry out the duties allocated to the Fireman under Rule 188 after satisfying himself that the fire is being dealt with.

When there is a fire, Drivers and Guards must act according to the best of their judgment and ability in the circumstances.

After ensuring that the fire has been extinguished, the small metal tab on the front of the fire alarm control box should be pulled off. This will uncover a switch which should be operated to stop the alarm bell and extinguish the warning light. It will also render it impossible to re-start the affected engine and after this has been done the train can proceed.

The alarm isolating switch referred to does not cut out the re-setting thermostat and should this operate through a recurrence of fire on the engine or fluid flywheel, the alarm bells will ring and the warning light will be lit. In this event the fire will not be extinguished automatically as the extinguishing agent will have been previously discharged. It is essential, therefore, for the remaining hand operated fire fighting equipment to be used as a matter of the utmost urgency after the train has been stopped.

The fire extinguishing agent used in the auxiliary power-cars is Chlorobromomethane. The vapour given off from the liquid is heavier than air and will therefore tend to settle at ground level but will be dispersed rapidly if there is a free current of air. Therefore an extinguisher going off normally in service is unlikely to constitute a hazard. Chlorobromomethane is not highly toxic and no dangers are likely to arise. Should an extinguisher be discharged accidentally and persons sprayed with the liquid in an enclosed space, the following simple precautions should be taken:-

1). Remove patient from the discharge area into the fresh air. Apply artificial respiration if necessary.

2). All clothing soaked by the liquid should be removed and where the liquid has splashed on the skin it should be washed off with water or, if available and the skin is not broken, by a saturated solution of bicarbonate of soda.

3). If the liquid enters the eyes wash freely with water.

4). Summon medical aid as soon as possible, notifying the doctor that the patient has been in contact with Chlorobromomethane and that oxygen therapy may be required.

5). If the liquid enters the mouth give the patient an emetic, such as one pint of saturated solution of bicarbonate of soda.

6). All clothing contaminated with the liquid should be laundered before being used again.

9. DEADMAN'S PEDAL

A Deadman's pedal is provided in all driving compartments and should the Driver release the pressure, the power will be cut off and the brakes applied.

10. DRIVING APPARATUS DISABLED

In the event of the driving apparatus in the leading compartment becoming disabled, and the Driver being able to regain control of the train from the other driving compartment the train must be driven at a reduced speed of not more than 15 m.p.h. from the most convenient driving compartment and proceed with caution to the nearest point where the train can be taken out of service. In such cases the Guard must ride in the leading driving compartment, keep a good look-out, operate the warning horns when necessary and practicable, and be in a position to stop the train as required by application of the hand brake. The Guard must carefully observe all signals and signal to the Driver as may be necessary in accordance with the bell codes shewn in Instruction No. 6.

11. ASSISTING DISABLED TRAIN

In an emergency, disabled Diesel Pullman trains can be assisted by any type of train or engine, but in such circumstances the trains must be worked cautiously and at reduced speed.

When a Diesel Pullman train is being assisted, the working must be in accordance with the special instructions included in the Driver's handbook and according to the type of train or engine which is providing the assistance.

In the event of an air brake defect the Guard must be prepared to ride in the rear driving compartment and operate the hand brake under the direction of the Driver as may be necessary.

Each Diesel Pullman train is provided with a draw hook at each end.

12. DERAILMENTS

In all cases where Diesel Pullman cars are derailed they must be rerailed only under the supervision of and by Running and Maintenance Department staff.

13. FLOODING OF THE LINE

The movement of Diesel Pullman trains is restricted during flooding of the line as indicated in the Weekly Permanent Way Notice (K2/530) and the Regional Appendix, dated 1st October, 1960, page 89, as for Diesel Electric Multiple Units.

C. W. POWELL,
Operating Officer.
August 1960

APPENDIX

Extract from:
British Railways (Western Region) Multiple Unit Diesel Trains.
For the information of Railway and Pullman Car Company Staff

TRAVELLING TECHNICIANS

A Travelling Technician from the Chief Mechanical & Electrical Engineer's Department will form part of the train crew of each train. He will travel in the leading Guard's compartment, in which a small cupboard for his tools and equipment has been provided. He will be responsible for:-

(i) Deciding which of the auxiliary engines should be used.

(ii) Changing over auxiliary engines en route.

(iii) Switching on the second auxiliary engine when requested by the Pullman Car Conductor during excessively cold weather.

(iv) Taking action when "fault" lights appear.

(v) Dealing with technical faults in traction equipment upon request from the driver.

(vi) Supervision of connection and disconnection of "shore" electrical supplies. Where provided at terminal points.

CARRIAGE CLEANING

The following carriage cleaning arrangements are applicable to the Diesel Multiple Unit Pullman trains:
EXTERIOR
Standard arrangements for British Railways Stock.
INTERIOR
Daily:
Vestibule, lavatory and corridor floors, using diluted suitable disinfectant. Chrome fittings wipe with damp rag. Empty Ash Trays at end of each day, and at the end of each individual journey during the day.

Weekly:
Carpets and upholstery, vacuum clean and remove stains as necessary.
Toilet walls (plastic), sponge down and dry off.
Aluminium fittings, dust off and clean with lanoline.
Fortnightly:
Plastic panels, i.e., saloon ceilings, second class partitions, sponge down lightly with clean water and dry off.
First class partitions (wood veneer), clean and polish with a good furniture polish.

Lanide panels (body sides and table tops), sponge down using a diluted solution of soap flakes or similar detergent, dry off with clean cloth.
Note: Acids must not be used for the cleaning of Pullman Cars.
The Pullman Car staff is responsible for equipping the lavatories with toilet rolls, soap, hand towels and the provision and changing of antimacassars in the Cars.

ROUTE RESTRICTIONS

These trains are built to the C.1 loading gauge with the exception of the traction motor gear cases which are to the L.1 gauge, and may work over running lines and sidings normally used for coaching stock, subject to the restrictions shown in the appropriate instructions.

STATION STOPS

In all cases, owing to the use of a standard formation, the trains should come to rest at the same position every day and this will enable the station staff to assist passengers in taking up a position as near as possible to the entrance of the coach in which their seats have been reserved. Station stops and turn-round times have been kept to a minimum consistent with the duties to be carried out and it is essential, therefore, that station staff and train crews should do all they can to avoid delays.

Next page: Brand new, and over the pit! Probably recorded at a time when testing was being undertaken and no doubt at the works of Metropolitan-Cammell. From being the centre of attention by the engineers in 1959 and 1960 to less than 15 years later when it would be the turn of the scrap-merchant. "Temora mutantur nos et mutamur in illis" – times change and we change with them.

(British Film Institute)